LOCAL AUTHOR

SEP 03

~104   **DATE DUE**

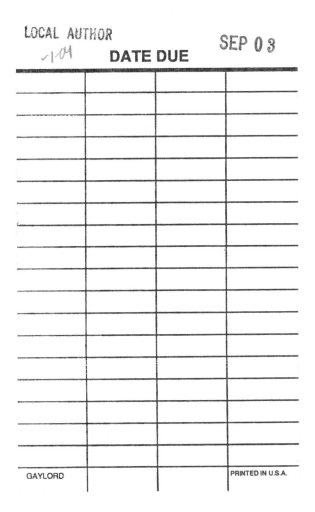

GAYLORD   PRINTED IN U.S.A.

Da Nang to Memphis

by
Linda G. Moreau

DORRANCE PUBLISHING CO., INC.
PITTSBURGH, PENNSYLVANIA 15222

ISBN # 0-8059-4794-9
Printed in the United States of America

First Printing

For information or to order additional books, please write:
Dorrance Publishing Co., Inc.
643 Smithfield Street
Pittsburgh, Pennsylvania 15222
U.S.A.
1-800-788-7654

To Nick, Laurie, Brian
and my two precious grandsons,
Travis and Hayden,
with love.

Contents

Introduction

I was just twenty-two years old when I was informed of my brother's missing-in-action status.

He had been in Vietnam for almost a year, and it was time to come home. His helicopter was shot down just fifteen days before the end of the war. Before this he had written home and told us he had married a Vietnamese woman with a three-year-old son. He sent pictures too. I was so anxious to meet his bride and welcome her and her little boy to our family.

Everything changed in a blink of an eye. Our lives were changed forever. I lost my brother, my sister-in-law, and her little boy. I was devastated.

It took twenty-three years to gather the strength, courage, determination, knowledge, and support necessary to make my dream come true. I wanted to find the woman that my brother loved. I wanted to go to Vietnam and say good-bye. I wanted to find a positive amongst all the negatives of war.

My dream came true, but I did not do it alone. I had support and love from all over the country. There is not a shortage of "beautiful people" in the world.

I wrote this book to encourage others to follow their hearts, to never give up, and most of all, not to be afraid to reach out.

Chapter One

Army Brats

On April 28, 1948, the ambulance sped across the Golden Gate Bridge to the maternity ward at Fort Baker. Because the maternity ward at Letterman General Hospital in Presidio, San Francisco, was not completed, Mickey was born across the bay.

By the time I came along on February 16, 1950, Letterman General Hospital's maternity ward was complete. Twenty months later on October 14, 1951, Sandra was born at Letterman. Then "Baby Jackey" arrived at Letterman on March 9, 1954.

Siblings, friends, companions, and sometimes enemies, we would soon learn to depend on each other during our childhood trekking around the world with our father, who was enlisted in the United States Army.

We left San Francisco in 1955 when we were 7, 5, 3, and 1 1/2 years of age. Mom had her hands full (to put it mildly), traveling alone with four little ones. As she told us frequently, Mom was very proud of the fact that she received many a compliment about her well-behaved children. As was customary in the army, an enlisted man traveled abroad first and sent for his family upon acquiring appropriate living quarters.

The four of us became very close during the three years we spent in Germany. It was our first trip out of the country. We were in a foreign land surrounded by unfamiliar faces, playing in the snow for the very first time, trying to communicate with people whose language was different from ours. It was both exciting and frightening and was to become our way of life. We looked to one another for support, confidence, and friendship. There was no television, so we entertained ourselves.

Upon returning to the United States in 1958, we were stationed at Ford Ord, California. Leaving Germany was hard after three years; we missed our friends, our teachers, and our neighborhood. The one and only consistent thing in our life was our household. We were thankful we always had each other. We traveled as a close-knit crew. No matter where we went, we always had companions. We made new friends and adjusted to our new environment rather quickly. We were a distinct brood.

After three years at Fort Ord, it was time to move on. This time we were destined for France. Oh, how we cried when we had to leave our friends and family again. It was 1961. I was 11, Mickey was 13, Sandy was 9, and Jackey was 7. Dad had once again traveled ahead of us, and when he rented a house in Nancy, he sent for his family. This journey was not quite as smooth as the first one even though we were much older. After traveling across the United States, our flight left from New York just as it did in 1955. Not long after takeoff, Sandy started to shriek and hold her ears. It was almost certain that she had an ear infection. The plane made an emergency landing in Newfoundland so Sandy could receive medical attention. What did we do to deserve this?

The little square ambulance with the Red Cross on the side met us at the aircraft and rushed us off to the hospital. How embarrassing! After Sandy's condition was diagnosed, we were escorted to the guest house. A guest house in a polar hellhole was not our idea of fun. We spent ten days there, and I believe we almost drove poor Mom crazy. We fought, argued, and protested the entire time. We really were army brats.

Before Dad left Nancy for the four-hour drive to Paris to pick us up, a message was to be delivered to let him know that we were not on the flight. But he did not get the message and he was frantic when we did not arrive in Paris as scheduled. Dad drove back to Nancy and was assured that he would be notified when we were due to arrive in Paris.

Yes, you guessed it–ten days later when we got off the plane in Paris, no one was there to pick us up.

Mickey, Linda, Sandy and Jackey (ages 9,7,5 and 3)
(1957 - Germany)

After a terrifying ride around Paris, we boarded the train to Nancy. At last we were almost home, where we would ultimately be reunited with Dad.

Our final destination was an enchanting, old, three-story house right in the middle of downtown Nancy. It had a coal furnace in the basement, a bathtub with feet, and a toilet in a closet all by itself with a chain hanging from the tank on the wall to flush it. I loved that house. Sandy and I slept on the third floor all alone. We never went up there alone though because it was so scary. Every night after we kissed our parents goodnight, we would cling to one another and run up the stairs as the lights flickered. We were such babies. The houses on our street were adjoined just like the houses in San Francisco. The only way to get to the backyard was through the dark, musty basement. Mickey got a great deal of pleasure out of scaring us. He was the only one who was not spooked by our new home. He was 13, a teenager, but we were just youngsters.

We learned to speak minimal French while we lived in Nancy. It simplified the task of ordering our delicious, fresh-from-the-oven French bread. Nothing will ever come close to the aroma and taste of that bread!

Our own, little private school bus would pick us up outside our door every morning to take us to Toul Army Depot. Dad took the car everyday and reported to duty in Toul while Mom remained home alone. Communicating with the neighbors was almost impossible because they spoke French, and Mom had very little in common with them. I didn't learn until adulthood that Mom was so unhappy and lonely in Nancy. She never let her feelings show. Her unhappiness lasted for fourteen months, and then we moved into Army quarters in Toul. There Mom was with all the other army wives again.

After a year in Toul, we were transferred to Verdun for our final year in France. We left France via the U.S.S. Upshur in 1964 bound for San Antonio, Texas. We were at sea for ten days. I always had a fear of water, but for some reason, I loved the cruise home.

We cried when we left France, but our tears were short-lived as usual. In Texas we adapted to our new life just as we had always done in the past. Now we were 16, 14, 12, and 10. The army brats were growing up.

Our San Antonio tour lasted three years and then Dad received his orders for Vietnam. He fought in WWII, was wounded twice, and met Mom in an army hospital while he was recuperating (she served her time during the war also). They married when he was released. I could not believe the Army would send him off to fight another war. Not my dad, please, not my dad!

Cousin Doug was already in Vietnam. I was seventeen, and most of the boys in my class were headed for Vietnam. By this time, Vietnam was a household word. It still is today and will always be a part of our lives.

Dad left in October of 1967, and we moved to California for the year that he was away. I was a senior in high school. We lived near Moffitt Field Naval Station. It was peculiar not having Dad around the house. I wrote to him often. I missed him and I worried about him every day. I watched the war on television.

In May of 1968, Doug returned from Vietnam. He was from Michigan, but he stopped by to visit us in California before going home. He visited Dad a few times while he was in Da Nang and Dad was in Qui Nhon. It wouldn't be long before Dad would be home. After all, Doug came home, so I knew that Dad would return home safely too. How naive I was then.

In June of 1968, I graduated from Sunnyvale High School, but Dad was not there. I did not have many friends in high school. I was shy and kind of a homebody, having found civilians a bit stuffy. I preferred to go to school with army brats.

In July of 1968, I met and fell in love with a sailor stationed at Moffitt Field. His name was Nick, so I thought initially. "Nick" turned out to be his nickname. Three weeks later when he asked me to marry him, I accepted. I wrote to Dad and told him all about Roland J. Moreau, the man I was going to marry in October when he returned from Vietnam. But Dad was not delighted to hear that we were getting married. I was only eighteen and Nick was nineteen, and we hadn't known one another very long. He said that his heart would not be in the wedding, but we waited until he returned and got married in the little chapel at Moffitt Field California on October 19, 1968.

Mickey had joined the army while Dad was in Vietnam. He was home on leave from boot camp when Nick and I got married. Sandy was my maid of honor. The wedding was small and simple, with an outdoor reception at Grandma and Grandpa's house.

The day after our wedding, my family left for Fort Lee, Virginia. Mickey stayed for a few days, and then he left to begin his career as an army helicopter pilot. We knew where that would lead him, but we never talked about it. He wanted to fly, and there was no stopping him. All four of us had the same stubborn streak.

It is now February 5, 1969, and Nick and I had a three pound, three ounce baby girl, Laurie, born two months prematurely. She was so tiny, so beautiful. Nick had already gotten his orders for the Philippines. He would be leaving in March. Laurie was due in April, but I guess she wanted to see her dad before he left for a year.

Laurie was still in the hospital when Nick departed from Travis Air Force Base. My world was turned upside down and inside out. I was 19, a wife, a mother, and alone. I did not know how I was going to survive the next year without Nick.

Just two days after Nick left, Laurie was released from El Camino Hospital weighing 4 pounds, 13 ounces. Then I knew how I would survive. This tiny baby took up every moment of my life. She needed me! We stayed in California for about a week and then flew to Fort Lee, Virginia, to be with Mom, Dad, Sandy, and Jackey. It had only been a few months since I last saw them, but I missed them terribly. Three out of four army brats were together again.

Laurie and I flew up to Connecticut to meet Nick's family. I had never met any of them. Nick had eleven brothers and

Last photo taken of all four of us (ages 20, 18, 16 and 14)
Sunnyvale, California, 1968.

sisters, six of whom were still living with Mom and Dad Moreau. We had a good time during the three-week visit, but then it was time to go back to Virginia. Nick wanted to live in Connecticut when he got out of the navy, so we knew we would see each other again soon.

Mickey was stationed near Washington, D.C., while we were in Virginia. He came to visit a few times, and one time Mom, Sandy, Jackey, Laurie, and I went to visit him and tour our capital. Mickey loved his little niece. He was not afraid to hold her and feed her. He would make a great dad some day. He always had wanted children.

Orders for Fort Carson, Colorado, arrived and my family would have to report for duty in July. They dropped me off in Connecticut at Mom and Dad Moreau's house and continued on to Colorado. Laurie and I lived with Nick's family until December of 1969. Nick got out of the navy early although he hadn't been due home until March 1970. We were glad to have him back. We didn't know it at the time, but Mickey, Sandy, Jackey, and I would never be together again after we left Virginia.

Nick, Laurie, and I made our home in Bantam, Connecticut. Mom, Dad, Sandy and Jack were in Colorado, and Mickey was still near Washington, D.C.

Mickey visited the family in Fort Carson once before Dad got orders for Germany again.

My parents loved Germany and wanted to go back one more time before their retirement.

The two remaining army brats were not thrilled. Sandy was eighteen and out of school, and she was not going to Germany. Mom and Dad took her to Detroit to stay with family while they were away.

Nick, Laurie, and I drove to Detroit to see the family before everyone went their own way. Mickey did not make it to Detroit. I'm not really sure where he was at the time because he was training for some special night-flying techniques.

Mom, Dad, and Jack left for Germany, and Sandy stayed

Mickey training for Vietnam
(1970 or 1971)

behind alone. It wasn't long before she took off and went back out West. Eventually she ended up in Hawaii. Sandy called Nick and me to talk about moving to Connecticut, but she opted for Los Angeles, a more fitting and exciting place for a single young woman.

Jack was very unhappy and restless in Germany. All he wanted to do was go home. He got his wish and was sent back to the United States. He was 17, I was 21, Sandy was 19, and Mickey was 23. Jack lived with Nick, Laurie, and me for a few months before moving to Louisiana to live with a friend.

Mickey visited us as often as he could. He loved to come up and spend time with Laurie and Nick's younger brothers and sisters. He had an orange VW convertible that the kids loved, and Mickey was never too busy to give them a ride.

In February 1972, Mickey called and asked, "Haven't you had that baby yet?" I was nine months pregnant; he was surprised to find me still carrying his nephew. We talked for a few minutes, and then Mickey asked for Mom and Dad's phone number in Germany. He wanted to call and let them know he would be leaving for Vietnam in a few days. Mom and Dad would be returning to the United States soon, but not soon enough to see their son again. I cried and Mickey made fun of me as usual. I told him that I loved him.

I never talked to my brother again. I was grateful for the opportunity to tell him that I loved him. I really thought that he would come home just like Dad and Doug.

On February 18, 1972, Nick and I were the proud parents of an 8 pound, 4 ounce baby boy, Brian. He never got the chance to meet his Uncle Mickey although I sent pictures of him and Laurie to Vietnam.

My parents returned to the United States in the spring of 1972. They went to Texas for the routine retirement procedures. Dad had been in the army for thirty-two years. While in Texas, they purchased a motor home. They had always wanted to travel around the United States when they retired. The "Golden Years" had arrived while they were still so young. Life was good.

Back in Connecticut, Nick and I purchased our first home. This would serve as the retirees' home base while they toured the country. They met their grandson for the first time in November 1972. Mom and Dad visited for a few days and then were off again. They had places to go, things to do, old friends to look up.

Periodically, Mom and Dad would call and ask me to send their mail to them. After my package with their mail arrived, they would move on. This system worked quite well.

On January 1, 1973, we broke the news to Nick's family that we were selling the house and moving back to California. We had been in Connecticut for almost four years now, and we both preferred the West Coast. The next month the kids would be one and four years old. We wanted to get settled before they started school.

On January 10th, I had put the kids to bed and was looking forward to watching a TV movie. Nick was on the phone with the realtor regarding the sale of our home. I saw lights in the driveway and then heard a knock on the back door.

I opened the door to a man in uniform. He asked for my father. Oh, an old army buddy, I thought. I invited him in and began to tell him the story about the wandering retirees, but he just stood there expressionless. When I looked into his eyes, I knew why he was standing in my kitchen. My legs were not gong to hold me up any longer. I felt myself sinking to my knees and started to sob, "Not Mickey, Not Mickey!" Nick hung up the phone and tried to comfort me, but he was in just as much pain as I was. Mickey was supposed to be home next month with Mary, the Vietnamese woman he said he had married. He had written to us and told us all about her. He had even sent pictures, and I was so excited about meeting my new sister-in-law. This couldn't be happening. The war was almost over. There had to be a mistake

Mickey was the commander of a UH-1H helicopter that was shot down in Quang Tri on January 8, 1973. After forty-eight hours, all six men on the helicopter were declared Missing in Action.

Mickey leaving for Vietnam
(February 1972)

I wish I could remember that officer's name. He was so kind and sympathetic. I still have the handkerchief that he gave me that night. I feel some strange sort of attachment to Mickey when I touch it.

Arrangements had to be made to tell my parents. They were on their way to Sandy and her fiance Carl's wedding in Los Angeles. I would not let them find the motor home on the highway and notify Mom and Dad. They had to wait until they arrived at Sandy's. I did not want them to be alone when they received the most devastating news that any parent could ever hear.

After a couple of hours, the officer left and the phone rang. It was my mother! I ran upstairs and locked myself in the bathroom. I remember sitting on the edge of the toilet rocking back and forth and banging my head on the sink so I could not hear the conversation that was taking place downstairs. Nick spoke with Mom for a while and then she asked to speak to me. Nick told her that I was at a Tupperware party. I don't know how Nick managed to control his emotions. I have always admired his strength. I think we were both in shock.

I don't really remember the rest of the night, but the morning of January 11, 1973, is when reality set in. More officers called and came out to the house. However, I was not the next of kin and was not the person that should have been notified. There were papers to sign, telegrams to read, and the all-to-real possibility of my parents calling again. I could not stay in that house alone! Nick took the kids and me to Mom and Dad Moreau's house every day for a week while he was at work. I was so afraid to answer the phone and so afraid that I would find out that Mickey was dead. We still had hope that he would come out of the jungle so Mom and Dad would never have to go through what we were going through

This was not a bad dream. This was real.

Laurie (3 years) and Brian (4 months)
Photo sent to Mickey in Vietnam
(June 1972)

Chapter Two

Missing in Action

Around January 16, 1973, Mom, Dad, and Sandy were notified of Mickey's status. They, in turn, called Jack and family to let them know.

Sandy and Carl's wedding was planned for January 20, 1973. Dad insisted on keeping the news quiet (we still had hope) and continued with the wedding plans. Every time I see Sandy and Carl's wedding pictures I can see the pain. I often wondered if everyone at the wedding saw it.

Our house sold rather quickly, and we made plans to move back to California. How I missed my family and needed to be with them then more than ever. We never talked about what happened January 8, 1973. The telegrams said that the helicopter crashed but did not burn. That vision haunts me to this day. We still had hope.

The Paris Peace Accords were initialed by U. S. negotiator Henry Kissinger on January 23, 1973, to come into effect four days later. There would be an exchange of prisoners, a cease-fire based on territory held, and withdrawal of all remaining U.S. troops from the south within sixty days. Then Mickey could come home. I was sure that he was alive, but they just couldn't find him. They didn't find Mickey, the other five men in the helicopter, or the helicopter itself. They only had fifteen days to go, and they had vanished!

Laurie and Brian don't know how much they helped me through this devastating period of my life. They made me get up every day and gave me the strength to get through the long, dreaded days. Nick was always there for me, but someone in the family had to work. At night I would sometimes stand in the dark looking out into the backyard picturing Mickey's face. It seemed so real. I was only twenty-two, but had learned the lesson of a lifetime: Live every day like it will be your last!

But the Prisoners of War were coming home! Mickey had to be one of them.

I was wrong again. Sitting on the floor in front of the television day after day, I watched every single POW get off the planes. I stared at each and every face. Sometimes I really thought I saw my brother and would lean closer to get a better look. I didn't know who I would notify when I found my brother among the faces, but that was not a concern at the moment. I was gladdened to see all those men come home to their families, but I was nauseous at the same time. I watched the reunions, the tears of joy, and thought I would be sick. None of this made any sense to me.

Attempts were made to locate Mary, but with all the chaos of war, she could not be located. Not long after my brother's incident, my thoughts shifted towards Mary. This poor young woman. She had a three-year-old son that Mickey was supposed to bring home too. What would happen to them? What if Mary was pregnant, and Mickey's child was still in Vietnam? These thoughts ran through my head constantly. I never uttered a word to anyone. These were my own private thoughts; someday I would find out I had to. I owed it to Mickey; he gave his life for us so I will take care of his family. It upset me to think Mary must think that we didn't care. I started having dreams of a little Vietnamese girl. I didn't know if it was Mary or Mary and Mickey's daughter. She always appeared and disappeared just as quickly. Vietnam was always on my mind.

It always amazed me that no one else in the family ever wondered about the possibility of Mary having Mickey's child. Maybe they were thinking it, but they felt as helpless as I did, so there was no point in bringing it up. I have always believed "where there is a will, there is a way."

Knowing someone is "missing" is a fate worse than death. One day you have hope, but then the next day you are so down you don't think you will ever have hope again. You cannot grieve. You cannot have a good time without feeling guilty. You cannot put it to rest. It haunts your every waking hour and sometimes your dreams too. I guess that's why we never really talked about it. It was too painful. What if Mickey was a prisoner? I know some of our men were left behind even though we were told they had all been returned. What happened to them? How long after January 8, 1973, did my brother live, and what kind of life did he have? Sometimes I would pretend that Mickey and Mary found each other and were living in seclusion with their children. Mickey was happy. The next day I would think of Mickey as a POW being tortured, starved and dying a lonely, horrible death. Why? Why? Why did this happen, and why can't it be over? The only way to protect ourselves from the anguish was to refrain from talking about it. We only talked about Mickey as we remembered him. The unknown was unbearable.

We arrived in California in April 1973. It was so good to be back. I had not seen any of my family since we lost Mickey. Just being in California made me feel close to my brother. Everywhere we went reminded me of him.

We went to Grandma's house. Mom and Dad were staying in their motor home in the backyard. They had been there since January, waiting for news of Mickey. But nothing had changed. He was still missing in action. We still had hope though.

When I saw my parents I thought I would collapse. I sobbed when I saw the pain in their eyes and could feel the pain in their hearts. When I looked at them, I saw Mickey. Inside Grandma's house, I could see Mickey. Mickey was everywhere. We had spent a lot of time together in that house when we were children. Grandpa had died while Mickey was in Vietnam. That house felt so cold and empty. I never enjoyed going to that house again.

Nick and I bought a house just down the street from the house that we lived in when Dad was in Vietnam. Mickey's memory was everywhere. They were good memories, and we all tried to be thankful for the twenty-four years that we had him with us. But I could never let Vietnam and Mary wander off very far. Mickey was counting on me.

Mom and Dad stayed nearby for a while and then took off in their motor home. They checked in often, just in case news came. They were using Grandma's address now as their home base. Mickey had always used Grandma's address.

Sandy and Carl moved from Los Angeles to San Jose. It was great having my little sister close by again. Jack and Lois were still in Louisiana. They had two little ones, Nick and Sandy. I had never met Lois and the kids, and it had been a while since I last saw Jack. I needed to see my little brother.

Life went on. Mickey would have wanted it that way. Mom and Dad continued to travel, and the rest of us absorbed ourselves in work and raising our families.

Laurie, Brian, and I went on a motor home trip with Mom and Dad to Louisiana and Texas with a stopover in San Diego on the return trip. Nick joined us there for a few days before we all rode home together. It was great. The kids still talk about that trip. We were pretending to be normal people again. Seeing my little brother was bittersweet. I wanted to see him, but he was in the army now and reminded me so much of Mickey. The pain just never went away. But we still had hope.

I had never been religious and now I knew why. If there was a God, this would not be happening. Why would he take Mickey? How could he cause this much pain?

Mickey just out of boot camp
(1968)

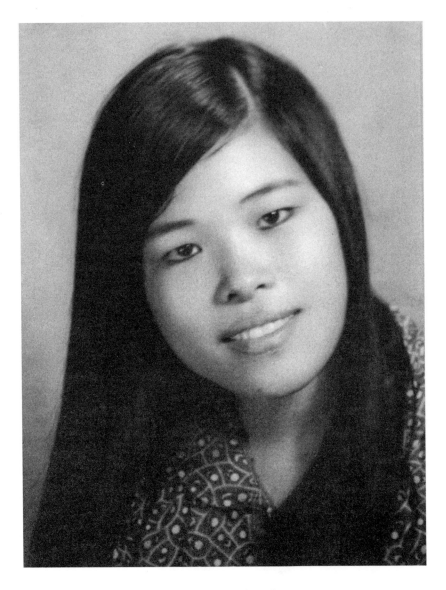

Mary Hong Thi Chau
The photo that Mickey sent home (1972)

Mary's oldest son Lam,
her Vietnamese son that Mickey was to bring home.
(1972)

Chapter Three

Life Went On

The crate toured the world in 1973 before reaching its final destination. Sometime in 1974, the crate, containing everything we had left of Mickey, arrived from Vietnam. Its yearlong journey took it from Vietnam to Germany to Connecticut before reaching Grandma's house in California.

Mom and Dad were living in the motor home in Northern California for a few months. They were trying to decide where to buy a house and settle down when I told them that Mickey's belongings were at Grandma's. The crate was brought to our house and stored in the garage until my parents purchased their first home.

I walked by that crate every day when I went to the garage to do the laundry. I would look at it, touch it, and wonder what was inside. Sometimes I even wondered if he was inside. I knew that was insane, but I couldn't help it. No one had any idea where Mickey was or what had happened to him. No one could just be missing! Maybe there would be a clue in that big wooden crate.

Mom and Dad took the crate to their new home. I don't know when they opened it. They said there was not much inside. Letters, some clothes, a small refrigerator, a helmet, a Bible, and various other personal effects were all we had left of Mickey. A Bible, how interesting. I hadn't known that Mickey was religious. What else was there to learn about my brother? How had he changed since I last saw him? Mickey the man, the soldier, the pilot, the husband, and maybe even a father. I only knew Mickey the child, the teenager, and the big brother.

Questions, all unanswered, filled my mind. I just could not

tolerate the unknown. But, on the other hand, I really did not want anymore bad news. Life went on and so did our sorrow, heartache, and bewilderment.

We moved several times while we were in California before moving to Medford, Oregon, in August 1980. Sandy and Carl had two children, Shana and Bradley, and they moved to Portland, Oregon, not long after we left California. Eventually they settled in Port Orchard, Washington.

Jack, Lois, and family went to Germany for three years while he was in the army. Jack had spent the majority of his life so far in Europe. Soon after returning to the United States, Jack and Lois divorced. Jack remarried and got out of the army. His new wife was Bonnie, and they had two children, Jackey and Jessie. We lost touch with Jack several times over the years. Sometimes it felt like both of my brothers were missing in action. I wanted my brothers back.

Sandy and I became increasingly close. We had been four army brats, and now there were two. How fast the years go by.

Mickey was promoted from WO1 to WO3 during his missing years. This always seemed very odd to me. He received a paycheck too. Mom and Dad received a Congressional Commemorative Medal in honor of Mickey in 1984. They also received monthly notices or visits from the army to let them know that Mickey was still missing.

It was extremely difficult to put the past behind you when it was constantly being brought to your attention. Every few months, an article would appear in the newspaper or on television about some "remains" being found and sent to the lab in Hawaii. Thousands of families around the country would be holding their breath for months while the remains were being identified. I thought this to be another cruel and torturous practice. Every time I heard about another set of remains, I would feel sick inside and hope that the rest of my family did not hear about it.

On October 5, 1978, under the provisions of Sections 555 and 556, Title 37, United States Code, and upon direction and delegation of authority by the Secretary of the Army, the Adjutant General found Mickey to be dead, remains not recovered.

He was presumed dead only because they could not prove him to be alive. He is still missing in action, but now he will no longer get paid. I guess it had to be done sooner or later. Our hope is fading. Only fading, not gone.

In December 1978 we had a memorial for Mickey at the Presidio. All the relatives were there. It was beautiful. The Twenty-One Gun Salute, Taps, Mom and Dad being presented with the flag. It was all so proper, so military, just like us. Mickey had sacrificed his life for us. He was a hero and should be honored accordingly. All our men were heroes. Through Mom and Dad's heartache and sorrow, I could see the pride.

Mickey has a white, marble headstone in the MIA section of the cemetery that overlooks the San Francisco Bay. We also had a bronze plaque placed in the brick walkway just outside the chapel. The army brats were all together one last time, in spirit only.

I visit the Presidio whenever I go to San Francisco. We were all born there, so it is a fitting place for us to remember Mickey as he was. He would love the view. It is so peaceful and beautiful and military. Even now, after the closure, the Presidio still has the look and feel of a military establishment. I could stay there for hours and get lost in my thoughts and tears and laughter. It is our home. Mickey had intended to make the military his career, just like his father. Someday I hoped to bring Mary to the Presidio.

I miss Mickey so much.

As the years went by, my thoughts of Mary and my dreams became more and more vivid and recurring. I had always wanted to go to Vietnam. I wanted to see the crash site and wanted to talk to Mary. She was the person that Mickey spent the last year of his life with. I wanted to find her, to touch her, to talk to her. I didn't know how I was going to accomplish this seemingly impossible task, but where there is a will, there is a way.

I needed to go to Vietnam because Mickey was still there. He would know when I was there. I was starting to believe in

Nick, Laurie, Brian and Linda in Hawaii
(1987)

something. I just wasn't sure what it was. I had a feeling inside that was guiding me to Vietnam. Maybe the feeling was from Mickey. He knew that I could do it. Nick had always been so supportive of me. Mickey must know that Nick will help me. I am sure that my big brother is looking after me, protecting me, and guiding me.

In May of 1995 I made the decision: I was going to Vietnam. I called a few local travel agencies for estimates. No one knew anything about traveling to Vietnam. I had not told Nick about my decision yet. I thought he would think I was crazy. I had no idea how much work would be involved in this trip. It was to become a labor of love. When I told Nick about my desire to go to Vietnam, he looked at me and said, "If that's what you want to do, then that's what we will do." How did I find this gem of a man? He never ceases to amaze me. He jumped right in and started helping me to plan the journey of a lifetime. I love him a little bit more every day. And they said it wouldn't last!

I called my sister and told her of our plans. Sandy said that I wasn't going without her and Carl. I knew she would feel that way, and I needed her to be with me. Sandy is part of me. The four of us were going to Vietnam to honor and thank Mickey and all our fellow Americans that served our country. This venture would consume the next year of our lives.

A friend of mine told me that it would take months to plan a trip to Vietnam and accomplish what I wanted to do. He told me to write letters to anyone I could think of that may be able to help me. I needed to find out where the crash site was; I had to find an L 7014 military map and learn how to read it; I needed a guide in Vietnam; I needed someone I could trust; we needed a visa and a passport to travel to Vietnam; and I needed advice.

Writing the letter was difficult, but I finally put one together. I asked for assistance both here and in Vietnam. I requested information regarding accommodations, guides, van rental, and assistance in finding Mary. I mailed and faxed my letter to

Veterans organizations, the Department of the Army, and travel agencies both here and in Vietnam. It was June 1995.

This friend of mine was so instrumental in planning and organizing my trip. I will never forget his advice, concern, and genuine friendship. He gave me a few ideas, and I ran with them.

Sometime in August after a conversation with the Department of the Army, I mailed them a request to receive a copy of Mickey's file and map of the incident location. It had to be sent to my father because he was next of kin, and then it was forwarded on to me. I received the file in October.

In my quest for knowledge, I was introduced to a Vietnamese woman named Mai. She had come to the United States in 1972 as the wife of an American serviceman.

Mai encouraged me to find Mary while others tried to discourage me. She always told me that my sister-in-law would be happy and grateful to know that I was looking for her. Some Vietnamese women gave their Amerasian babies away, fearing they would be accused of sleeping with the enemy. Some women and children did not survive the war and some were lost at sea trying to flee the country. Mary might have married a Vietnamese man and she may have hidden the fact that she was involved with an American. Exposing her now could be dangerous and devastating.

Mai never let me believe any of the negatives. We had to hope that Mary and her children were some of the lucky ones.

I'm sure that Mai does not realize what an important role she has played in my life. She is my link to a world that I long to learn about. Through our long and meaningful conversations, I began to understand why my search for Mary was so difficult.

Vietnamese people are not preoccupied with dates, times, certificates, and documents. They are concerned with survival, not what day and time an incident occurred. Most Vietnamese people cannot afford a watch or a calendar. Even if they could, not much need existed for them. They work in the fields from sunup to sundown seven days a week just trying to survive.

So many people in Vietnam have changed their identity for one reason or another. The mothers of young girls who were nearing the "fighting age" had their daughters' birth certificates destroyed. New names and dates of birth were issued, therefore buying a very precious commodity: time. After 1975 many mothers with American babies burned everything they had that could connect them to the enemy. They feared for their lives and the lives of their children.

Mai never saw her mother again after she left her country in 1972. Her mother is buried not far from where my brother's helicopter was shot down in Quang Tri. Her uncle still lives in Quang Tri. The world is really a small planet. We told Mai that we would visit her uncle and her mother's grave while we were in Vietnam.

With each meeting, we became more and more aware of just how grateful Mai was to be an American. She made me think of Mary. I knew that Mary would be like Mai. What an asset Mary would have been to our family. I felt guilty for not trying to find her sooner and saddened for all the lost years.

Mom and Dad were worried about us traveling to Vietnam, and I don't really think they understood why we had to go. Dad told me to do what I had to do and not to let anyone stand in my way. I never wanted to upset my parents, but I had to do this. I had been holding back for twenty-two years. I needed answers, and they needed peace of mind. We all needed Mickey to come home, dead or alive, but it wasn't happening.

Originally the only purpose of my trip was to say good-bye to my brother, to go to the crash site, to spend some time in the country in which he perished. Finding Mary was an after-thought. I didn't even know her Vietnamese name. I just thought I would try to locate her while I was in her homeland.

Mickey's file was enormous, ten file folders filled with volumes of information about his entire military career. I read every line. It took weeks and many tears, but I read and stud-ied every word. I found out that Mary had a real name, Chau Thi Hong, Hong being her first name. I was exhilarated! I had a clue. I was very optimistic, but my optimism was often criticized.

From Mickey's file I learned the location of the crash site. I read the military map and located the general area on the map of Vietnam that I had purchased. Nick and I spent every evening and weekend working out the details and watching videos and documentaries about Vietnam and its people. I did not want to read about the war; I wanted to learn about the people, their customs, and their beliefs. This would help me project what Mary might have done after she lost Mickey.

From Mickey's file I learned that he wore glasses while flying. I have copies of his dental records. The flight schedule was the hardest for me to read. It listed the time and date of every flight he took while he was in Vietnam. His signature was on almost every piece of paper in the file. Difficult as it was to read the file, it is a part of Mickey's memory that is very dear to me. I feel like I shared his last year with him.

One day my friend called and asked me if he could give my name to the *Mail Tribune*. He thought my quest would make a good human-interest story. I didn't see any harm in sharing my learning experiences with others. Maybe I could be of assistance to someone in a similar situation. A couple of weeks later, a writer called and asked me to come in for an interview.

I liked the reporter immediately. In November 1995 my article was in the local newspaper. I was speechless. The picture of Mickey was so big, and the article practically consumed the entire page. It warmed my heart to know that people still cared about our missing soldiers. This article would be one of many that he would write about Mickey.

One day a Vietnam veteran from Seattle called after receiving one of the letters I had mailed. He had accompanied groups of veterans returning to Vietnam after the war. He had been back twelve times, and now offered his assistance to us. He was a blessing.

He told us what to expect and what would be expected of us. I had received correspondence from a couple of Vietnamese travel agencies. He verified their reputation before we made a selection. We were getting so excited because everything was falling into place. We planned to leave for Vietnam on April 6, 1996. It seemed so far away, but we needed the time to prepare. So much work still needed to be done.

One day I read an article in the *Mail Tribune* about the Living Memorial Sculpture Garden in Week, California. I asked Nick if he would like to take a ride down there and have a look at it, so we did. The garden consists of many sculptures honoring groups of war heroes. All the sculptures have names: *The Refugees, The Why Group, POW-MIA, The Flute Player, Those Left Behind, The Peaceful Warrior, The Korean War Veteran Monument, Coming Home, The Nurses,* and *Hot LZ Memorial Wall,* which is a place for remembering the 2,188 helicopter pilots who died in Vietnam. They will never be forgotten. This garden will never be forgotten by anyone who has the privilege of visiting its grounds. It is breathtaking with Mount Shasta in the background. Nick and I walked around and, of course, shed some tears, something we do frequently these days.

On the way out, I saw a brochure about the Vietnam Helicopter Pilots Association (VHPA). I just looked at it and put it down. Nick suggested I go back and get it and write to them because someone in the VHPA should know who Mickey was. Why didn't I think of that? I guess two heads are better than one.

In September 1995 I wrote to the VHPA and asked if anyone knew Mickey in Vietnam or before he went to Vietnam. I also subscribed to their newsletter. My letter appeared in December 1995/January 1996 VHPA Newsletter!

The first person to respond to my letter was a Vietnamese poet. I received a package from him on January 8, 1996. January 8th was the anniversary of Mickey's incident. Coincidences like this are happening more and more often. I really think Mickey has something to do with it. The package contained a card and twenty dollars to buy some flowers or incense for Mickey. There were copies of newspaper articles about the poet and his family and their accomplishments. There was a copy of one of his poems enclosed called "Dear Daddy" that he wanted me to read to Mickey at the crash site. This man was only 19 years old when he came to America as one of the first refugees to land at Camp Pendleton, California. As a child in Vietnam, he befriended a helicopter pilot who eventually was killed. He never forgot the pilots who fought for his freedom. He has used his talents as a poet, speaker, and artist to dedicate his life to thanking America. Nick and I were so moved by his kind, sincere, generous, and loving gestures.

Chapter Four

Voices From His Past

My journey to Vietnam would not have been a success had it not been for all the wonderful, kind, and generous individuals that reached out and touched me. The telephone opened up a whole new world, Mickey's world.

The letter I had written to the VHPA generated quite a bit of interest. I was actually shocked to know that there were so many people out there who cared. It's a warm and comforting feeling.

On January 18, 1996, I heard the first voice from Mickey's past. I was told that he, two other pilots, and Mickey were all stationed together in Fort Belvoir, Virginia. The foursome had flown all over the United States while training for special night-flying techniques to be used in Vietnam.

He and one of the other pilots had returned from their tour of duty just three months before Mickey left for Vietnam. Neither one knew what had happened to Mickey until they read the letter in the VHPA. They assumed Mickey was alive and well. I felt horrible for upsetting them. Mickey's good friend said that he had called the other members of the foursome as soon as he read my letter. He gave me his address and phone number.

"Mickey was a man of tremendous character," he said. Mickey was liked and respected by everyone. He said that Mickey was the most popular crew chief. He was responsible and dedicated. Yes, that was my brother!

The VHPA hosts an annual reunion every Fourth of July that lasts for several days. The reunions are held in different corners of the United States to enable all members to attend. Maybe we would meet at a VHPA reunion some day.

My heart was racing as we said good-bye and hung up. I

was so elated to have talked to one of Mickey's friends, although it was very emotionally draining. I sat on the couch and cried. Oh, Mickey, why did you have to go? We all miss you so much.

I received a fax from another pilot that day who said he was involved in the rescue attempt. He asked me to call, but was not in when I returned his call. We had to play phone tag for a few days before we finally spoke.

On January 19, 1996, another voice was heard. This pilot was in Da Nang during Mickey's tour of duty. He did not know him very well, but he remembers the day he was shot down. "You just never forget things like that," he said.

His purpose for calling was to give me the names of some men that knew Mickey quite well. He gave me several pilots' names and the states in which they had retired. These men knew how to keep in touch and remain good friends. The next day I called information and got the phone number of the men he had mentioned. This man was shocked when I told him who I was and why I was calling. He remembered Mickey very well. He referred to him as "the blond-headed young fellow." Mickey had looked younger than he was. He was twenty three when he went to Vietnam; granted twenty three is not old, but a lot of our soldiers were still in their teens.

He remembered Mickey as being an excellent pilot with a great sense of humor. He told me this story. One night while Mickey was on a support mission, he ran low on fuel. He landed the helicopter on a sand bar and got it stuck. The crew removed the doors and machine guns to lighten the aircraft, but it was so dark they could not continue. Their only option was to wait until daybreak. When the crew woke up, the helicopter was gone! It was so light, it had floated down the river as they slept. The helicopter was never recovered. The crew was rescued.

I love that story. I could just picture the look on Mickey's face and hear the laughter. I was grateful to know that there was laughter.

He and Mickey were in the same unit in Da Nang. He knew nothing about Mary and said that he did not know when Mickey would have had time for a woman because he had worked ten to fourteen hours a day, seven days a week.

He suggested I find Mickey's Commanding Officer and talk to him. Just hearing all the military talk brought back memories of the army brats. How I missed us then.

On January 20, 1996, I received a fax from another friend of Mickey's. I returned the call immediately.

He and Mickey flew many missions together in Vietnam. His tour of duty ended prior to Mickey's incident. This is what he had heard about January 8, 1973: he was told that Mickey was shot down north of Quang Tri. He was forced down onto a road and was last seen being led away from the aircraft at gunpoint. All eyewitnesses were South Vietnamese. I had never heard that before. It was difficult to hear, but I appreciated his honesty.

He knew that Mickey was sweet on Mary but did not know that they had married. All the girls that worked in the clubs were very nice and sincere, he said. They all flirted with them but were discouraged from dating them, much less marrying them. His memory of Mickey was as a bit of a daredevil and an excellent pilot. He always felt safe when he flew with Mickey.

He suggested I call Mickey's platoon leader. We recalled the floating helicopter incident and laughed together. He said he would go to Vietnam with us in April if he could. I was in the process of designing a marble monument to be placed at the crash site, and he wanted to be there for the dedication. He said he would send money to help defray the cost of the marker.

What a friend. A few days later a check for $100 arrived. I cried about everything, but they were tears of joy.

The pilot who had called a couple of days earlier about the rescue attempt called back. It seems that he was stationed about forty-five minutes away from Quang Tri from September 1972 until March 1973. He flew to Mickey's crash site about three hours after it was reported. He could not reach the aircraft because the area was completely enemy-occupied. He said that no American ground troops were available and the only eye-witnesses were South Vietnamese.

The floating helicopter story came up again. He told me that Mickey's unit called themselves the "Coachmen."

By March 28, 1973, all American troops were out of that area, the pilot included. Being a member of the VHPA for some time, he gave me a little background on the organization.

He told me of a friend of Mickey's who was still in the army who was now stationed at Fort Lewis, Washington. He gave me his name and suggested I give him a call.

The VHPA has an annual directory which lists a brief description of what happened to our missing pilots. This is what the VHPA said about Mickey's helicopter incident: The helicopter was flying low due to bad weather when it flew over the demilitarize zone (DMZ) into enemy territory and was shot down. The Army of the Republic of South Vietnam (ARVN) saw the North Vietnamese Army (NVA) capture the crew, Tail #69-15619. They mentioned other crew members as a cross-reference.

Sometimes I wondered why I was putting myself through all this. It was all so emotional and difficult. Nick was always close by to share my sorrow and my happiness. The word bittersweet kept coming to mind. All told, I was very grateful and honored to hear from the voices from Mickey's past.

January 20, 1996 was Sandy and Carl's twenty-third wedding anniversary, Mickey had been missing for twenty-three years.

One more voice was heard that day. This call was the most shocking. This man did not know Mickey, although he was in Da Nang at the same time.

He was retired from the army. About a week earlier, he had dinner with an old army friend that he had not seen in awhile. His friend brought along one of his friends. He did not know the third individual, although all three men were in Da Nang at the same time.

During dinner the topic of conversation centered on January 8, 1973, and Mickey's incident. The third individual said that he had delivered Mickey and Mary's baby! None of the men had received the December/January volume of the VHPA Newsletter yet.

The VHPA Newsletter arrived a few days after the dinner. When this man saw my letter, he called immediately to tell me about what had happened at the dinner. He promised to find the mysterious third party and have him call me. This was one remarkable human being.

My dreams all these years had so much more meaning. How did I know that Mickey had a child? My heart felt like it was going to explode. I didn't know what to do with this information. Nick and I sat and discussed it for awhile and tried to calm down. It felt like 1973 again. I was carrying a heavy load. I had to call Sandy.

Sandy began to cry, and then we both cried. We were absolutely astonished. The more we thought about what had just occurred, the more unbelievable it became. This was a dream come true. Why were all the puzzle pieces falling into place now? I knew that Mickey would be pleased and proud if he could see me now.

I did not receive any more phone calls on January 20. I don't know if I could have survived any more calls. What I needed was time, time to think and digest everything I had learned that day.

I wished we could find Jack. It had been several years since anyone had heard from him.

On January 22, 1996, Sandy called the man at Fort Lewis. She lives close by and volunteered her support. It seems that he did not know Mickey, he just knew of the incident. He said that they were putting together a search team when it was reported that the pilots and crew were seen being led away by the North Vietnamese Army (NVA). The search was called off. He wished us well and said that we could call anytime if there was anything he could do.

On January 24, 1996, I came home for lunch and found a message on my answering machine. The mysterious third party had been located. I had his work phone number, which I called, but he was not in so I left a message for him to call me as soon as possible.

By January 26, 1996, the third part had not called me back. I called my friend and left a message asking him if he could find his home phone number.

I called information and got the phone number of Mickey's Commanding Officer. He was very surprised to hear from me. He was not a member of the VHPA. He got very emotional when he talked about Vietnam. I apologized for calling, but he said it was all right. It was not my intent to upset anyone. He was in Da Nang when Mickey was shot down, and this is what he was told of the incident.

Mickey's helicopter was off course, but no one knew why. He was flying low, as instructed. He must have popped up to see where he was when he was hit by a heat seeker missile. The aircraft was seen with binoculars by U.S. personnel. The South Vietnamese saw all six men standing beside the aircraft.

I asked him what he thought happened to our men. He answered, "You know what I think. Don't make me verbalize it." There was silence, then tears. Not another word was said on the subject. It was not necessary.

He went on to tell me about the Army Aviation Museum in Fort Rucker, Alabama. Mickey and the other five men on the helicopter are honored there. I knew I would have to go to see it someday.

I asked if he knew about Mary. He said, "Of course," he was Mickey's Commanding Officer. He said that he had met Mary once. It was his job to try to talk soldiers out of marrying Vietnamese women, but Mickey was totally immersed in his relationship with Mary. Mickey loved her and was absolutely determined to marry her, he said. It was his duty to discourage such a union, but when he realized there was no changing Mickey's mind, he wished them well and helped them with the appropriate procedures.

Mickey and Mary did get married. He thought they got married at the consulate, but he was not certain. He thought one of the other five men on the helicopter that crashed January 8, 1973 also had a Vietnamese wife.

I asked if he knew if Mary was pregnant or not. To the best of his knowledge, he said he thought she was pregnant. I did not tell him about the baby. I wanted confirmation of the information I received a few days earlier. He remembered Mickey as being quiet, kind of a loner who worked hard and did his job well. Mickey was with Mary whenever he was not working. He and his wife said they envied us for taking the trip to Vietnam. They would like to go someday and then continue on to Australia.

My optimism was growing by leaps and bounds. And so was my phone bill.

On January 30, 1996, the mystery man called me at work! I ran to a phone where I could have a little more privacy. I knew this would be emotional. Being both a helicopter pilot and a medical officer, he said he had helped deliver quite a few Vietnamese-American babies. He believed Mickey's baby was a girl. It was a long time ago. I could not believe I was talking to the man who held my brother's child. I tried to picture the scene in my mind. He told me that others were present: a chaplain, another warrant officer, another medical officer, and some Vietnamese Nationals. He promised to try to get the names of the other Americans who were present. He gave me his home phone number, fax number, and pager number and told me to call anytime, day or night. We said good-bye and hung up. I was emotionally and mentally exhausted. I went home to compose myself and get some rest.

I called Sandy and broke the news: "I think we have a niece." We wondered about her name, her looks, and her whereabouts. She would be 23 years old now. Maybe she has children. Could Mickey be a grandfather?

Your mind can take you anywhere if you just open it and let it go. The possibilities are endless. The future was looking brighter. Mickey lives. I just needed to find the life that Mickey left for us.

So many Amerasian children were left behind after the war. My brother had a family in Vietnam. He married the mother of his child and had every intention of bringing them home and providing for them. He loved them. Fifteen days, only fifteen more days and they would have been here where they belong. Mickey fought for his country; I will fight for his family.

On February 27, 1996, another friend of Mickey's left a message on my answering machine. I called him back as soon as I could. His wife answered. We talked briefly, and then Mickey's friend got on the phone.

He said that he loved Mickey. Mickey had lived with him, his wife, and their two little sons in Paso Robles, California, for six to nine months while they were training. Being a young married couple with two children made it difficult to find time and money to go out. Sometimes Mickey would watch the boys, which allowed them the privilege of an evening out alone. Mickey was part of their family.

This man was the fourth team member of the crew that flew around the United States while training for Vietnam. They were all in the same unit of which Mickey was the crew chief. He told me that Mickey was a wonderful man, and as an E5 crew chief, he flew as well as any seasoned pilot. They always had a lot of fun flying everyday.

We talked and talked and talked some more. This family has so many memories of my brother.

They had tried to locate Mickey many times over the years, but the Military Locator said they had no records of him. They thought that Mickey had gotten out of the army and was living somewhere in the United States with his family. Of course, nothing could be further from the truth. He and his wife were devastated when one of the other men from the team called to tell them that Mickey was missing in action.

They said they envied us for taking the trip. He wanted to return someday. He told us to keep an open mind. We shared some tears that night;it was March 9, 1996, Jack's forty-second birthday. I wondered where he was.

The phone calls had slowed down a little, but on this day yet another voice was heard. A friend of Mickey's read my letter in the VHPA Newsletter and told him to call. He and Mickey were in the same division but did not know one another. He was a Chinook pilot, and Mickey flew Hueys.

His wife was Korean and they lived in Washington. He told me about several Vietnamese communities in the Tacoma area, where they have a very large temple.

There were three officers' clubs in Da Nang. He also told me that Mary was a very common nickname that the girls used because the Americans could not pronounce their Vietnamese names. "Kim" and "Lee" were also common.

Everyone who called had a different reason for doing so, and each and every one of them had so much to offer. If it were not for the VHPA and their dedicated members, I would still be searching and wondering today.

A few days later, Nick and I hopped in the pickup camper and headed for Washington. I made a flyer with pictures of Mickey, Mary, and her three-year-old son that asked for information regarding their whereabouts or anyone who might think that they knew them. Someone had to know them, especially if they were in the United States.

We spent the weekend handing out flyers at temples, Vietnamese markets, jewelry stores, travel agencies, restaurants, and any other Asian-looking establishment. We went all the way to Seattle. It was a long shot, but it was all we had. Mickey probably would have laughed about that little caper.

Later on March 9, I received a call from yet another one of Mickey's friends. He said he knew Mickey and knew about the baby. He thought the baby was born before Mickey was shot down. He never met Mary, but he said it was common knowledge that she had been pregnant.

A few years ago he wrote an account of the crash incident for the VHPA. It went like this: The weather was not very good, which made it difficult to see the landmarks the crew used to guide them while flying. Mickey must not have been able to see the landmark, resulting in a missed turn. He ended up in enemy territory. He also heard that they were all seen standing outside the aircraft.

He also suggested I talk to Mickey's platoon leader. If I reached his platoon leader, he wanted me to ask him to call. This man seemed to think that this platoon leader would have a lot of information about Mickey.

That day, I found Mickey's platoon leader. He told me that he completed two tours in Vietnam, and when he left, he left it behind and never thought about it. He was not upset that I called. He did not remember Mickey; he did however, remember Mickey's friend. I gave him the message that I was asked to give.

On March 17, 1996, I received a fax from the man in Washington who told me about the temple. He ran a database search of some Vietnamese organizations here in the United States and sent it to me. There were almost one hundred names and addresses including churches, temples, stores, restaurants, youth centers, and other facilities.

We would be leaving for Vietnam shortly, so I would follow-up with the organizations when I returned. I was impressed.

On March 25, 1996, the man that gave me the phone number of the mystery man called again. He found the name of Mickey's company chaplain in Da Nang. Maybe he was the chaplain who was present at the birth of Mickey's child.

On March 26, 1996, the writer from the *Mail Tribune* wrote another article about Mickey and our upcoming venture to Vietnam. I didn't know if I was ready to go, but by then I didn't really have any choice.

I received a call from a very sweet and kind woman who told me about a Vietnamese family that her family had hosted many years ago. They were settled in California but kept in touch. She told me the Vietnamese here in the United States have a very special network for staying in touch. She asked my permission to send my article to her Vietnamese family in California in hopes that they might be of some assistance. Of course I said yes. Her son, also a Vietnam veteran, was from Channel 12 News. We watched him every morning. What a small world.

On April 3, 1996, the chaplain called. He knew Mickey very well but was not the attending chaplain at the birth of Mickey's child. He told me that Mickey borrowed his jeep to go to see Mary, but said if he had not given it to him, Mickey would have walked. Mickey was the only man over there that he knew who had a life and tried to be normal. He never drank or ran around with the guys. He was always with Mary when he was off duty.

On April 5, 1996, I realized we would be leaving the next morning. I couldn't sleep. At 10:00 p.m. we received a fax from our Vietnamese poet friend. He had written a poem for Mickey. He wanted me to read it to him at the crash site. I put the poem in my purse with his poem "Dear Daddy." Then I was ready to go.

Chapter Five
Vietnam 1996

I called my parents to say good-bye before we left for Vietnam. My father said, "You make damn sure you come home." I knew what he was thinking about.

We were buckled into our seats and ready for takeoff and some shut-eye. It was 4:00 A.M. but I could not sleep. My mind was too active. What were our boys thinking when they took this journey? How did they feel? What was going through their minds? I couldn't stop thinking about the war and the effect it had on our nation. My chest felt tight and my stomach was in a knot as Nick and I left the runway and flew out across the sea as so many Americans had done before us. They were leaving to fight for us: we were leaving to thank them.

Sandy and Carl had gone ahead of us to spend a couple of days in Thailand. We would meet at the Rex Hotel in Saigon on April 8, 1996.

All the months of planning, all the anxiety, and all the dreaming had come to an end. We were on our way. The passengers consisted mostly of happy, content Asians going home to visit family I presumed. When I looked around the aircraft, their faces looked like frightened soldiers. I knew it was just my imagination, but that did not make the vision subside.

Outside the clouds were white and fluffy. Flying above the clouds always made me think of heaven. I could see Mickey; he was not alone. He was with his comrades. I had been dreading the long flight, but actually it was not as bad as I had expected. We landed in Taipei for a short layover, and then we were on our way to Saigon.

While waiting for the passengers ahead of us to depart, we

looked out the window and saw Vietnam. I cannot explain how I felt that day. The sadness was pushed aside by my happiness to be so near Mickey.

We had a smooth flight and a fairly smooth trip through the airport formalities before we were thrust into the reality of Vietnam waiting outside. The airport was fenced off to locals. The scene reminded me of the pictures I had seen of hundreds of Vietnamese trying to flee the country before Saigon fell into the hands of the North. People were lined up on the other side of the fence with their faces pushed into the wire. They were yelling, waving and some were crying. Many were holding signs displaying the names of tourists. We found our name and our guide. They were not allowed into the airport to greet the arrivals. How odd and frightening at the same time.

How I wished that I spoke their language. My heart went out to them. This was a time of peace; I tried to imagine it during the war.

Saigon is a noisy, bustling and thriving city. Our guide was a lovely, gracious, young Vietnamese woman named Kelly, not her real name of course – just another easy to pronounce and easy to remember nickname. Some things never change.

We toured the city briefly before arriving at the Rex. We were exhausted, but our excitement gave us our second wind. Kelly would have to take the van and driver back to the airport to pick up Sandy and Carl in a couple of hours. Nick and I opted for some free time.

After a quick freshening up, we were out of our room exploring the Rex. What a magnificent hotel so full of history. We had read about it before we left home. We went up on the roof and enjoyed the view of the city. It was a long way down to the street, but that did not muffle the sounds of the city below. The traffic in Saigon was the most entertaining thing I have ever witnessed. We were so anxious for Sandy and Carl to arrive and share all of this with us.

Finally, they arrived. We hugged and greeted one another as if we had not seen them for years. They were bright and refreshed. They just flew in from Thailand, a mere hop-skip-and-jump away. Nick and I looked like we had slept in our clothes – maybe that's because we had. Oh well, we had a lot to do. We hit the streets for a cyclo tour of the city. The drivers were very friendly and informative, but we especially appreciated their skill. Carl once made the comment that the cyclo rides were like a ride at an amusement park. How true it was. We had some close calls.

Nick and I had a difficult time staying awake once we sat down in the cyclo with the hot sun beating down on us. We toured for about an hour, returned to the hotel for an early dinner, and then opted for some sleep. Tomorrow we would return to the airport for a short flight to Da Nang where we would be met by our new guide and driver and taken to our hotel in Hue.

Kelly left us at the airport on April 9, 1996. We would be back to spend a couple more days in Saigon before heading for home.

The flight to Da Nang was an experience nothing like the United States. While we stood on the boarding stairs, the engines started. The heat was burning our faces and the exhaust was choking us. We looked at one another and had to laugh. They had no safety regulations. Once seated, the pilot announced that we were going to take off. The plane started to taxi down the runway while the stewardesses ran down the isle before being thrown into their seats. We were definitely flying at our own risk!

Miraculously, we landed in Da Nang safely. The airport in Da Nang was much smaller, quieter, and more orderly. Again we met our guide and driver outside the facility.

Our guide's name was Tin. He was very educated and polite, and his English was extremely good. The driver was one of those silent types. We never quite bonded with him, but he was an excellent driver and we appreciated his skill as much as we did the skill of the Saigon cyclo drivers.

We were to meet with the director of the travel agency while in Da Nang. I had been corresponding with him via fax for almost a year. He was to arrange for the building of the marble monument. I was to pay him cash upon arriving in Da Nang. He told me the project would be complete to include a picture of Mickey and the engraving.

Tin took us to the travel agency, but the director would not see me. His assistant informed me that the government would not allow the marker to be placed at the crash site. I was upset but I tried not to let it show. I felt betrayed. We left the travel agency and headed for the hotel. Tin suggested we stop at the market and order flowers tomorrow when we arrive in Hue. We had a quiet dinner before turning in early. Tomorrow would be a long day.

Upon arriving in Hue, we went to the market and ordered a huge wreath. We wanted the best, and the best cost us ten dollars. It would be ready to pick up tomorrow morning when we took the ride up to the crash site.

The hotel was beautifully located on the Perfume River. I soon forgot my disappointment and enjoyed the rest of the day. Vietnam was mesmerizing. We had another early dinner and retired shortly thereafter. Tomorrow we were going to the crash site. The anticipation was overwhelming; I did not sleep very well.

We were up early as usual and ready to go downstairs for breakfast. I was having a very difficult time with the food because I don't like rice, seafood, tea, or many vegetables. I had a stash of dried fruit and granola bars in case of an emergency.

Breakfast was in the form of a buffet. That was good news. Better news – they had pork and beans. I loaded up with beans, bread and coffee. I was glad that we would be staying here for a few days because emergency rations could be stashed away for a while longer. Tin and the driver never ate in the dining room with us. They were eating at a table just outside the dining room when we came down the stairs.

The waitresses were beautiful in the traditional Vietnamese ao dai. The long flowing tunics and wide leg pants were so flattering to their lean, petite frames and were complimented even more by their shiny jet-black hair. They looked like Asian Barbie dolls.

We took our seats in the van and headed for the market. The flowers were gorgeous! I could not believe all the work that went into that wreath and it was only ten dollars. Tin bought some incense to burn for Mickey. I do believe that his gesture was sincere. Carefully, Tin placed the wreath in the back of the van. It was almost too large.

We were on our way then. We would be gone the entire day. We were headed for Dong Ha to meet a local guide who would escort us to the crash site. It was quite a ride; the flowers held up quite well considering the heat, lack of water, and constant jarring of the van due to the poor condition of the road.

Mr. Chi, our guide, was quite young but seemed to be familiar with the area. We visited for awhile – no one seems to be in a hurry in Vietnam – before Mr. Chi joined us in the van for the final portion of our journey to the crash site.

We stopped along the highway and looked down a path that led to the Thach Han River. We had drawn a crowd as usual. Foreigners were not a common sight outside of the big cities. A group of school children had stopped to talk. They loved to practice their English. Carefully, the wreath was removed from the van and carried by Tin and Mr. Chi. The four of us followed single file along the long, narrow path.

It was extremely hot and humid in Quang Tri. We thought we would never see the river when finally it appeared before us. The wind came up as soon as we neared the water.

I looked to the right and saw the bridge that had been mentioned in the casualty reports as a landmark. I looked all around. We had finally arrived!

I could not halt the tears from pouring down my face. But I did not want to cry; I wanted to savor every moment that I was there. I wanted to visualize everything clearly so that I could store it away in my memory bank.

It was silent, but I could hear the helicopters overhead. I could see them. I could feel Mickey's company. I took a deep breath and then sealed the vault of my memory bank. No one can ever take this away from me.

Tin and Mr. Chi stood the wreath up and backed away. Sandy and I knelt in front of it and reminded Mickey of just how much we loved and missed him. Carefully unfolding the poems, we read them to our big brother. We choked on our words several times but we finally succeeded. It felt wonderful, tranquil, and momentous. All of us lit incense and stood it in the soil around the wreath and on the riverbank. The wind was very strong, causing the wreath to topple over a couple of times. Tin suggested we float it down the river.

Nick and Carl carried the flowers to the riverbank. We all bowed our heads and shared some private, silent moments with Mickey. The wreath was pushed into the current headed for the bridge.

The marble monument would not have been as memorable as this ceremony. I was pleased that the marker was never completed. Sometimes it is difficult to understand why things happen as they do, but there is always a reason.

The remaining incense was placed in various spots nearby. We watched as the wreath made its way downstream. Some local women coming back from the market stopped and stared with obvious curiosity. A few men had gathered around to talk to our guides. Everyone was genuinely concerned and respected our privacy.

It was peaceful and beautiful. We said one last good-bye before making our way back to the van. May all our soldiers rest in peace and beauty forever!

The heat was unbearable. The ride to Mai's uncle's house was welcomed because we needed time in the van with the air conditioner running. I'm sure that the emotion that had run through our bodies had an effect on our overheated condition.

We found Mai's uncle's house without any difficulty. He was not in the main house when we arrived. No one spoke a word of English, but it was obvious that Mai's uncle's family were thrilled to have us in their home. They brought out the fans and plugged them in and offered us some drinks while we waited for Mai's uncle. He walked bent over looking at the ground. When he saw us he stood straight as an arrow and smiled before returning to his comfortable stance. Many years of working in the rice fields had left him unable to stand straight.

Mai's uncle was delightful. He held my hand and bowed several times. He greeted the others with the same warmth and sincerity. Mai had sent vitamins, anti-diarrhea medication, pain relievers, and other medication for the family. They received them with genuine appreciation. The rainy season would be upon them soon and they would certainly need the medicine. Mai had to rewrite all the labels in Vietnamese so they would understand how to use them.

Mai also sent money. We were to give it to her uncle only. I had seen pictures of him, but the toddlers in the house proved to us that we were in the right place. I had brought a picture of us with Mai. When we showed it to the little tikes, they pointed to her and started yelling, "Mai, Mai!" We gave the money to Mai's uncle to be divided fairly amongst the other family members. It was such a rewarding feeling to see the looks on their faces.

We stayed and visited for awhile before taking the short ride up the road to Mai's mother's grave. One of the younger men in the house led the way. The grave was just as it had looked in the picture Mai had shown us. It is more like a shrine and was very colorful. They were in the process of adding Mai's mother's picture to the headstone. Mai had given the family the money to build the structure for her mother. Mai had never seen her mother again after she left in 1972.

Never a moment was wasted during our Vietnam tour. The guides kept us right on schedule and filled each day with interest, education, sentiment and entertainment. We left the gravesite to witness some absolutely gorgeous landscape as we headed towards the DMZ (the demilitarized zone). Vietnam is

Tin and Mr. Chi leading us to the crash site
(April 1996)

Linda and Sandy reading poetry to Mickey

Linda, Nick, Sandy and Carl saying good-bye
(April 1996)

Linda and Sandy lighting incense at the crash site
(April 1996)

Nick and Carl placing the wreath in the Thach Han River
(April 1996)

One last good-bye
"We Love You, Mickey"

Locals talking to our guides –
some of them said they saw the crash

one of the most beautiful, serene places I have ever seen. I especially loved the water buffalo because they were so powerful and majestic looking.

The DMZ – we had heard those three letters so many times – were not mere letters any longer. The war crept back into our thoughts just when we were starting to enjoy the peace and tranquility of this country.

The tunnels were not far away. Nick and Carl expressed a desire to tour them. While the men took a tour of the tunnels, Sandy and I took advantage of the free time to sit on the beach and visit with some of the local peasants. Well, we tried to visit with them. All they wanted to do was sell us a Coke, 7UP, or some bottled water. Everyone tried to make a dollar somehow. How heartbreaking to see little children selling to tourists. I could not imagine my children in such a situation.

It had been a long and very emotional day. On the way back, we stopped in Quang Tri. I saw a tiny figure get up out of a chair alongside the road. It was Mai's uncle! He sat and waited for us to drive past (he knew we would because there was only one road) so he could give us a package for Mai. I opened the window as he walked up to the van, and he handed me the gift of ginger and pepper he had grown and packaged for Mai. How long had he been sitting there? I will never forget his tiny, frail image as we drove away.

We returned to Hue for an excellent dinner and a good night's sleep. We had been through a lot that day. Tomorrow we would unwind and take in the sights.

Hue is a beautiful city which lies in the lovely countryside of the Huong Giang, the Perfume River. We toured the city and learned the history of Hue from our guide, Tin.

Tin was an expert on the history of the Vietnam War and loved to talk about it. We explored the Citadel of Hue, the Imperial Palace, the Thien Mu Pagoda (one of my favorites), the tomb of the twelfth Nguyen Dynasty Emperor, and the tomb of Tu Duc before taking a boat ride down the Perfume River. I felt like I had just walked through the pages of a history book. We all had a very educational and wonderful day. It was time to return to the hotel, have dinner, pack, and retire early as usual. We always had to be ready to go by 7:00 or 7:30 A.M.! Tomorrow we were headed back to Da Nang. Tin said the director of the travel agency wanted to have lunch with us when we returned.

The time we spent in that van was not always pleasant due to the condition of the roads. In Vietnam everyone uses the roads; they have no lanes, signs, or speed limits, but everyone has a horn and loves to use it. The road (basically there was only one we built during the war) was so full of potholes it was virtually impossible to go straight.

Everyone dodged holes, traffic, water buffalo, pedestrians, and rice drying along the way. I was amazed that we did not see any really bad accidents, although we were run off the road once. Our most experienced driver made a quick recovery, and we were on our way once again.

Da Nang, the capital of Quang Nam, lies on the Han River and on a large bay with a huge natural harbor filled with ships. Mickey and our cousin Doug had been stationed here while they were in Vietnam.

The director of the travel agency and his assistant met us for lunch at a waterfront restaurant. Both were pleasant but reserved. I tipped them for the time and effort they spent on our tour. They had faxed some information about Mary before we left home. (Later I would find out that their information included false leads) They promised to complete the marble monument if the government decided to allow it.

Our hotel was right on the beach. I knew that Mickey would have walked along this beach because he loved the water and the outdoors. I tried to picture him there. It was very quiet at this hotel with not many guests.

Cyclos and drivers were never difficult to find. One day Tin hired four drivers to take care of us and show us around Da Nang. The drivers were great. We drove by the old army base several times. I wish we could have gone inside, but it was off limits and was being used by the Vietnamese military. The walls of those old buildings could tell some stories. I wondered where Mickey called home while he was here. Where was the baby born? I knew the birthplace was just outside the walls of the base, but where?

As we toured the City of Da Nang, I looked at every man, woman, and child hoping to recognize someone, anyone. I stared at their faces just as I had stared at the faces of the POWs twenty-three years ago.

While in Da Nang we visited Marble Mountain, a convent, many marble shops, and the homes of Tin and the driver.

Our trip was nearing the end, but I did not want it to be over. So much work was left to do. Although Tin and the director of the travel agency vowed to keep looking for Mary after our departure, I knew I had to come back someday and pick up where we left off.

Next on our itinerary was the very scenic drive from Da Nang to Qui Nhon. Our accommodations in Qui Nhon were not up to the standards of the hotels to which we were accustomed. The city was smaller than Saigon, Hue, or Da Nang. We got on the military base without any problems after Tin handed the guard a pack of cigarettes. We were instructed not to take any pictures. My father was stationed here, so we took pictures anyway. We would be flying out of Qui Nhon tomorrow, using the military air strip that so many of our troops had used in years gone by. The war came back to mind.

Our Vietnamese poet friend was from Qui Nhon. We found his old house and took pictures for him. This is where he befriended his "Dear Daddy" helicopter pilot. He has never been back home since.

Tin and the driver picked us up very early the next morning for the ride back to the airstrip. I was going to miss Tin. Saying good-bye was very emotional. I cried when I hugged him. He did not understand American emotions. "You are very easily moved," he said, turning his head away. I think he was crying too.

Kelly met us at the Saigon airport and took us back to the Rex. Sandy and Carl would be leaving a day ahead of Nick and me.

Local women returning from the market in Quang Tri

Mai's uncle
(April 1996)

Mai's mother's grave, just down the street from the crash site

Tin and family:
His oldest daughter (left) is now going to school in West Virginia

I had read so much about the Mekong Delta before we left home that I just had to see it. Kelly arranged a tour for the four of us. It was just as I had imagined. We took a large boat across the river to a plantation, where we toured an old farmhouse and tasted all the exotic fruits of the region. Then we took small boats (similar to canoes) for a peaceful, beautiful scenic tour through the jungle. It was fantastic! It is so quiet and lush in the countryside of Vietnam.

We said good-bye to Sandy and Carl the next morning as they headed for the airport with Kelly. Time went by so fast; Nick and I only had one more day to spend in this country that had captured our hearts. We made the most of the time we had left by touring and shopping the streets of Saigon.

I never stopped staring into the eyes of every person that crossed my path. I was always on the lookout for Mickey, Mary, and their child. I have never said that my brother is dead – I just can't do it. I need proof. I guess I am an eternal optimist. Maybe I am just too stubborn to give up.

Nick and I had our last dinner at the Continental Hotel. They served great spaghetti! As we walked back to the Rex Hotel, I stopped and bid Saigon farewell. We would be going home in the morning.

While waiting for Kelly to arrive and take us to the airport, Nick told me about the dream he had the night before.

Nick said that he dreamt that Mickey knocked on our door last night. He knew we were in Vietnam, but he was just waiting for the right moment to come and see me. I had that dream too. Nick and I have been married so long that we even dream alike.

Kelly took us to the airport one last time. She had family in the United States and planned on joining them within the year. She cried as we said our farewells. We exchanged addresses and phone numbers, hoping to see her again.

As the plane lifted above the city, my heart fell. Good-bye Mickey – we will be back again some day, I said to myself.

Children at the convent in Da Nang

Linda, Nick, Carl, and Sandy at the fruit farm
along the bank of the Mekong Delta
(April 1996)

Chapter Six

Obsessed

The word "obsessed" was used quite often to describe my behavior. I was the first to admit that was true.

I'm a headstrong, obsessed, optimist, and it has taken its toll on everyone around me. I am truly sorry, but I couldn't give up.

Our trip was rewarding in so many ways, but as I looked back, I realized that I was nothing but a tourist. I felt like I had not done enough to find Mickey's family. I didn't know what else to do.

We had been home for a couple of weeks when a package from Carl arrived. He sent me a marble box containing two small, polished stones. He had collected stones from the crash site when Sandy and I were not looking. He had them polished and gave them to us as a souvenir to be forever treasured.

That list of Vietnamese organizations that was mailed to me became my text tool. I mailed a flyer to every address. Things started happening again!

One Vietnamese woman called to ask if I wanted to advertise on a Vietnamese radio station in Southern California where they have a very large Vietnamese population. It was fairly inexpensive, so I decided to give it a try. I never left any stone unturned.

I received an unusual letter a couple of weeks later. The letter was from a Vietnamese man in California. He said he had just moved from Houston, Texas, and knew a Vietnamese doctor there that had many patients named "Hong." He gave me the name and phone number of the doctor. Mai called him for me, and he agreed to try to find my sister-in-law. I mailed information and pictures to him.

On June 14, 1996, I received a phone call from Garden Grove, California. People here in the United States volunteer their time to help Amerasian children find their fathers, but I did not know this! This wonderful man called to open up his Rolodex to me. He gave me the names, addresses, and phone/fax numbers of several individuals and organizations that might be able to help in my search for my brother's child. I was as amazed as I was impressed.

If my brother's child made it to the United States, she might be looking for her father. I'm not sure if Mary knew what really happened to Mickey. The two might think he was alive. At this point in time, we really thought that Mickey had a little girl, so we were always looking for his daughter.

I contacted every person and organization on the list. Everyone was so helpful, and each one gave me the name and address of another contact. My network was growing. I had no choice but to succeed with all this love and support. I had help from California, Kentucky, New Jersey, Wisconsin, and New York. I had people placing ads in Vietnamese newspapers for me. These people understood my obsession because they had obsessions of their own.

Two men in particular became very special to me. One was from New Jersey, the other from California. They were very involved in helping the Montagnard people of Vietnam. The man from California was in Vietnam the same time we were. He went back to visit "his children" he had not seen since the war. I had never met any of these wonderful people, but I hoped to some day.

With my growing obsession came growing curiosity. I started to read books about Amerasians and Vietnamese people, and even some war stories.

I was invited to attend the VHPA reunion in Santa Clara, California. Nick, Sandy, and I decided to go. The couple that Mickey lived with in Paso Robles was going to be there. We would also meet our Vietnamese poet friend, his wife, and their

Nick and Linda on the Mekong Delta

three children. Maybe some other men who knew my brother would be there.

The reunion lasted for several days; we arrived on the Fourth of July. We found our Vietnamese poet and his family first. They had a table set up in the room designated for vendors. We had exchanged pictures, therefore we recognized them immediately. He and his family were tending to the display of his book titled *Dear Daddy*. He stood on a chair and serenaded us. What an extraordinary man!

A bulletin board in the lobby was used to post information of all sorts. I put a picture and information about Mickey on the board. I let everyone know how they could reach me.

We knew that Mickey's friends were here, but we kept missing them. It was easy to do when we did not know for whom we were looking. Messages of all kinds were left on the bulletin board or on the voice-mail system in hopes of connecting with a long, lost friend. The turnout for this function was amazing.

While in the lobby, a woman walked towards me, looked at me, and asked if I was Linda. I knew immediately who she was. We finally met the couple that Mickey had lived with in Paso Robles! They felt like family to us. We talked, laughed, hugged, and cried. It was easy to understand why Mickey was so close to them.

Someone else was looking for me. This pilot thought that he had gone to flight school with my brother. As it turned out, he did not go to school with Mickey but he knew someone at the reunion who did.

He found Mickey's classmate and brought him to us. This man knew Mickey from flight school. We visited and exchanged stories. He did not know what happened to my brother. I brought my pictures from our Vietnam trip and shared them with the pilots. Most of them had never been back to Vietnam and really enjoyed looking at the pictures. One of them said that Mickey was very lucky to have two sisters that would go all the way to Vietnam to say good-bye. He said that if it were done for him, he would be very happy.

If Mickey was alive, he would have been right in the middle of all of this. He would have loved it. It was an exhilarating experience. The men and their families were so involved and dedicated to preserving the memory of every Vietnam helicopter pilot. They had a special program before the banquet to honor the missing in action. It was the most touching display of love and gratitude I had ever witnessed.

I received another message that someone was looking for me, but we kept missing one another. I left a message for him including a description of myself and told him I would be in the room with the vendors.

It wasn't long before a man asked I was Linda. I said yes and he said, "I have something that I think you should have." He took the MIA/POW bracelet off his wrist and gave it to me. It was Mickey's! His arm was white where the bracelet had been. I put my arms around him and sobbed right there in front of everyone. When I dried my eyes, I told him that I would not take it off until I could put it on the arm of Mickey's child. He had come all the way from Oklahoma to give that bracelet to me. He read my letter in the VHPA Newsletter. I will never forget his kindness.

Prior to leaving Medford, I received a letter from the woman at the radio station where I had done some advertising. She gave me the name and address of a Vietnamese man in San Jose. He did not have a phone. He said he had some information about my brother, so Nick and I took the time to find him while we were in the area.

We found the man's apartment in a run-down neighborhood. We rang the doorbell and a tiny Vietnamese woman answered. She did not speak English, but she motioned for us to come in after I showed her the letter I had received.

Her husband was in the living room. The whole apartment smelled like urine. The poor little man was bedridden with kidney problems. He kept saying something about Oklahoma City and my brother. He seemed to be going in and out of consciousness and was not making any sense. He asked for my address and told me that he would send me something.

All the while his little wife was pacing round the room. She brought us a drink. We tried to be polite and drink it, but the stench of the apartment was getting the best of us. He said he had been there since June 1991. It was obvious that he was on his deathbed. We thanked them and said good-bye. We don't know what he wanted and were never to hear from him again. We went back to the reunion with a sick feeling. What was he trying to tell us?

The next few months were spent trying to locate Mary, her Vietnamese son, and my brother's child in the United States. There was a very good chance that they got out of Vietnam though the Orderly Departure Program (ODP). I knew nothing about this and many other organizations until the members of my network informed me of them. I felt ashamed – why didn't I know?

I wrote, phoned, and faxed to Interaction; *Southeast Asia Resource Action Center; *U.S. Committee for Scientific Cooperation with Vietnam; *Human Rights Advocates International, Inc; *Association of Military Surgeons of the U.S.; *Bureau of Population, Refugee, and Migration Affairs; *U.S. Department of State; * Australia Vietnam War Veterans Trust; * National Personnel Records Center; *East Meets West Foundation; *American Embassy in Vietnam; and the *Department of the Army.

My efforts were not successful in locating my brother's family. I kept reading and trying.

One Sunday as I was reading the paper, I saw an article in Parade Magazine. There was a picture of this family in Massachusetts who had adopted six children over the past twenty-six years. One of them was a young Vietnamese women who looked like Mary! I called information and got their phone number. The young Vietnamese woman answered the phone. I assured her that I was not crazy, but I had to ask her a few questions. She was very understanding. We talked for quite some time. She did not know who her mother or father was.

She had been adopted from an orphanage. She was not sure of her age either.

We compared notes and although not many similarities existed, I was not convinced that she was not my niece. She and her mother, and one brother, would be going back to Vietnam soon to try to locate their birth parents. I told her to call if she found out that her mother's name was Hong. She was a beautiful and intelligent young woman. We wished each other the best of luck.

By this time I knew that I had to return to Vietnam soon to continue my search. Mai's father was very ill and elderly so I wanted to see him, and my friend Ron from Channel 12 TV was a Vietnam veteran who wanted to go back someday.

It was also time to start learning about DNA. I knew that when I found Mickey's child, I would need proof.

A Vietnamese woman named Le Ly Hayslip had written two books about her life in Vietnam and in the United States. She went back to Vietnam to set up a clinic to help her people called East Meets West Foundation. Nick and I could not put the books down until we were finished; they were so fascinating. I called her to find out more about the foundation. Her strength and determination were so motivational.

When it came to DNA testing, I decided that Dr. Maples would be the first person I would call. I had heard about him, and he was one of the best in his field.

A friend of mine had given me a book called *Kiss the Boys Good-bye*. She told me that I might not want to read it, but she thought that I would benefit from it. Difficult as it was, I read the book. To say that it was thought provoking would be an understatement. The chapter about Ross Perot was of particular interest to me.

I had called the San Francisco-based office of East Meets West Foundation to get more information about the organization. I wanted to do something for the people of Vietnam. After all, they were my people too. One of the children that they helped at the clinic could have been my niece or nephew. The director told me that they used television in Vietnam to locate people. One instance he told me about was a man who needed a wheelchair. When they had finally found a chair for him, they had lost contact with the man. They advertised on the television and through word of mouth, the man showed up at the clinic to claim his wheelchair.

He suggested that I use the TV to locate Mary, but he cautioned that it might be expensive. What a great idea. I became very excited. I knew I could find her.

We decided to return to Vietnam in July of 1997. Mai would visit her father, Nick and I would work on finding my brother's family, and Ron from Channel 12 TV would visit Nha Trang (where he was stationed during the war) and cover our stories at the same time.

If at all possible, Nick, Mai, and I would accompany Ron to Nha Trang. Mai was not sure of her father's condition, and Nick and I might want to stay in Da Nang as long as possible in case someone had information about Mary.

I was not going back to Da Nang to find Mary; I was going back because that is where she was when the baby was born. I was positive that someone would come forward with a clue. That's all I expected, just a clue.

Prior to our 1996 trip, the director of the travel agency in Da Nang had faxed me some information about Mary. He said her date of birth was 12/12/47 and that she was from Quang Ngai. He also sent a small picture of her that looked like it was from an identification card of some kind. She looked very young. He also told me of her employment history with our government during the war. Then the information came to a halt. He said he would find out more but that was the last I heard of it. I think he used this information to coax me into using his travel services. He also told me that he had advertised in the newspaper and on television. "There was no response," he said.

One day I decided to call Ross Perot. I knew about his involvement in the POW/MIA issues, and I just wanted to talk to him. I called information and got his number. He was out of town when I called, so I left a message.

It was not like me to be so aggressive and assertive. Nothing seemed to stop me these days. I guess that's why I've been called "obsessed." I don't know when I changed.

A few days later, Ross Perot called me back. I like this man. He is so blunt. I appreciate honesty in any form. I told him of my plans to return to Vietnam. I wanted to know if he thought there were any living American soldiers left in Vietnam because I often wondered if Mickey had survived and maybe Mary knew where he was. I did not know if Mary had given the baby away, if the baby had died, or if it was left in an orphanage. I wanted to find out if Mickey and Mary really had been married. I had so many unanswered questions.

I told Mr. Perot that I was looking for Mary, her Vietnamese child, and my brother's child.

He told me to take my emotions out of it, but I could not do that. Then he told me to deal only in facts. When I found Mary, all my other questions would be answered. He felt I was wasting my time and energy by going in so many directions at one time, but he wished us well.

I knew only one thing for certain. I knew what she looked like because Mickey had sent us a picture of her and a picture is worth a thousand words.

I thought about what Ross Perot had told me. He was right. I must concentrate on facts. I did not know anything to be 100 percent accurate except that the picture was Mary because Mickey sent it home twenty-four years ago.

Advertising on television and in the newspaper was the only way to go. I was told that it had been done last year, but I had never seen it. I would do it myself; then I will know the truth.

A few weeks before we left for Vietnam again, a card from Seattle arrived. It was from a man who had been to Vietnam recently. He met a woman in Da Nang who had taken a week off from her job to try to find Mary for me. She had seen some of the information I had faxed to East Meets West Foundation. She did not even know me. Why was she so eager to help? He gave me her name and address and asked me to look her up.

She spoke very good English, he said, and her name was Tam. I would find her and thank her when I get to Da Nang, I indicated. I put the card in my purse.

There was so much kindness and goodness in the world. Why do we focus on the negative? The war was tragic, but because of the war, I have found so much love and understanding. I hope I can be strong enough to return the support to others who are in need.

Chapter Seven

Vietnam 1997

In June 1997 Sandy called to tell me that she found Jack and his family. They were living in California. Sandy and her family would visit Jack during the Fourth of July weekend. Nick and I would leave for Vietnam on July 3. A feeling of confidence overcame me. I was ready to go. I was ready for whatever came my way.

Saigon had not really changed in a year, but it seemed different this time. Was it because I was looking at everything differently?

Due to some confusion with our in-country flight, we remained in Saigon for a couple extra days. I was disappointed only because I wanted to get to Da Nang to do the advertising I had been planning. I loved spending time in Saigon. We took advantage of our days by sightseeing, eating, and shopping. We bought some beautiful furniture and souvenirs to be shipped home. Mai was the instigator of the shopping sprees.

I had read quite a lot about our Amerasian children and their plight. I was convinced that some still lived in Saigon. One day while we were out with the cyclo drivers, I asked them to take me to the American war children. Much to my amazement, they found them for me. They were afraid of us at first, but then they became very friendly. Some were black, some were white, some were Hispanic. Most were in their late twenties, outcasts living in solitude in their native land. I wondered if one of them was my brother's child. I wanted to take them all home.

We spent several hours in a dark and musty room with them. We held their babies and their hands. They gave us documents, birth certificates, pictures of their fathers, anything they thought might help them get to America. They thought we had come to help them. I promised to do what I could when we got home. I took pictures of them. A couple of them said that they would be going to the United States soon, which they confirmed by showing us papers from the ODP.

When we prepared to leave, one of the young women came up to me and sniffed the side of my face. Mai laughed at the look on my face. "That was a Vietnamese kiss," she said. I kissed them good-bye Vietnamese-style and then kissed them American-style. They kissed me both ways too, and we exchanged addresses. Leaving them was one of the hardest things I ever had to do. I wondered if their fathers even knew of their existence. Nick, Ron, Mai, and I headed back to our hotel with heavy hearts. The war was forever present in this peaceful country.

We had fun in Saigon, but we had work to do in Da Nang. One of Mai's uncles lived there, and her father and stepmother were staying with them. Mai was very anxious to see her father because his health had not been good. She hoped he would still be alive when we got to Da Nang.

Our flight north was short and uneventful. After finding a suitable hotel right on the river for twenty dollars a night, we all went to work.

Mai found her father to be in worse shape than she thought. We had brought some medication from home and hoped it would ease his pain. I think just seeing Mai again made him feel better. After a few days, he showed signs of improvement.

Nick and I located Tam. She was so helpful. She took us to the local newspaper and TV station. I still do not know why she took a week off to look for Mary. She said that when she had read about me, she felt sorry for me. Can you imagine – her feeling sorry for me?

Tam was in her early forties. She had one son and three nieces living with her. Tam's husband left in a boat headed for Australia about twenty years ago. Their son was just a baby, and

Two young Vietnamese girls leading me to the Amerasians!
(July 1997)

Linda holding an Amerasian grandchild.
(July 1997)

Ron and some local children –
they loved him! (July 1997)

Ron. Those little ones are not just Vietnamese.
(July 1997)

Thu-Ha, who now lives in Houston
(July 1997)

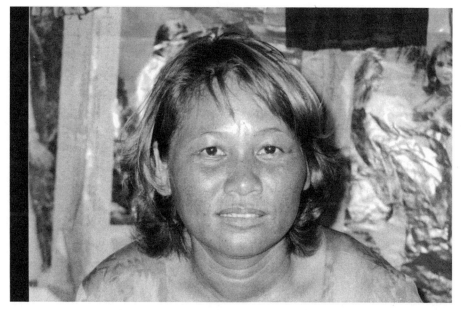

Another causality of the war – who is she?
(July 1997)

Two more women without a country
(July 1997)

They are certainly not Vietnamese
(July 1997)

Buddies – no one else wants them
(July 1997)

Some say she is too old to be Amerasian,
maybe it's because of her difficult life
(July 1997)

Tam was worried about his surviving the journey. Her husband left them behind with a promise to send for them when he got settled in Australia, but he never did. He is remarried and stayed in Australia.

Tam's sister could not take care of her children, so she had left them in Tam's care. Tam cooked and sold her goods on the street corner. One night Tam invited us all over for dinner. She cooked American food for us! She was very uncomfortable taking money from us, but we insisted. She said she did not help us for money. I really think she was sincere, but she did have mouths to feed.

Tam and Mai became friends. Every time we turned around, Tam was there on her motorbike. I was glad to see her take care of Mai. Her uncle lived so far away from the hotel and we worried about her making the trip alone at night.

Placing the ad in the newspaper was very simple. I just gave them $100 and it was done. The TV advertising was not so simple. We arrived in Vietnam on Saturday. We finally arrived at Da Nang on Tuesday. The newspaper advertising was done on Wednesday, ready to be on the newsstand the next day. The TV station said they had to check with the authorities before they could do anything. It would probably be Monday before they received an answer, and we were leaving on Wednesday!

Tam made arrangements for a van and driver to take us to Hue on Saturday. We would stay one night and return to Da Nang Sunday evening. I wanted to be at the TV station early Monday morning.

Mai's uncle and niece made the journey with us. They wanted to attend a wedding in Hue. Even though they did not speak one word of English, and Nick, Ron, and I did not speak Vietnamese, we had a great time. Mai was quite busy translating.

After settling in our hotel, Ron, Nick and I went for a swim. It felt so good. The weather was very hot and humid, and the pool was refreshing. Mai went on to her cousin's house. She would be back later to pick us up and take us back to her cousin's for dinner. Mai wanted to spend the night with her family

Linda and Tam (July 1997)

Linda checking out my article in the newspaper in Da Nang
(July 1997)

so that she could be with them as much as possible.

After the swim we went to the roof of the hotel for a light snack and breathtaking view. Our hotel was right next to the one that we had stayed in last year. The Perfume River was beautiful, ruffled only by the loud, obnoxious music coming from one of the boats.

While we were eating dinner at Mai's cousin's house, some of the children went to bed. They slept right on the concrete floor with no blanket, or pillow. Mai would do the same when everyone retired for the night. The baby was put to bed in a basket suspended from the ceiling in the kitchen. The house had no doors or glass in the windows. The animals came and went as they pleased. The family cooked, showered, and went to the bathroom outside. It reminded me of a very well organized family camping trip.

The driver drove us back to our hotel. Mai and some of her family would pick us up early the next morning for the trip to the market in Quang Tri, the crash site, Mai's mother's grave, Mai's uncle's house, her father's house (to see her half-sisters), and then back to Da Nang.

The next morning we were dressed, fed, and waiting for Mai. She was late, but it was not like her to be so late. We had no way of getting in touch with her. Worry was starting to set in when finally she limped into the restaurant.

She had made an early morning trip to the market on the family bicycle and had been the victim of a hit and run. We knew something was wrong. She was not badly injured, but she realized just how Americanized she had become. Even though we all laughed when we tried to picture the scene in our minds, we were aware of some of the dangers of being in a foreign country. We were so thankful that Mai was safe now.

The market in Quang Tri was very busy, but all came to a standstill when we got out of the van. Mai was afraid we would get mauled, but I wanted to buy some flowers for Mickey and her mother. The pickings were slim, but they had just what we needed. Mai ushered us back to the van, and we were on our way to the crash site.

Nick had no problem directing the driver to the crash site. It had been more than a year since we were in Quang Tri, but it seemed like it was just yesterday.

I jokingly expressed a desire to ride a water buffalo, but the joke was on me. As we walked down the path to the crash site, we came across a young boy and his water buffalo. Mai paid him to borrow the beast for a few minutes. Yes, I climbed up on the scratchy animal with my yellow dress pulled between my legs and rode the beast while my companions roared. It was a Kodak moment, a moment that Mickey would have enjoyed tremendously! It was the easiest money that young boy ever earned. He was bewildered at best.

When we arrived at the riverbank, our moods became solemn once again. I separated the flowers and handed everyone a small bouquet. Mai's family was so gracious. They bowed, said a few words, tossed the flowers in the river, and stood with their arms around me as I grieved. Ron, Nick, and I bowed our heads in memory of our soldiers. I knew that we were all there together, but it seemed more like a dream. I stood there in Vietnam with my friends and Mai's family. Mickey would be so pleased. He would like my friends, and I knew they would like Mickey if only they had had a chance to meet. If only his wife and child could have been there too.

Seeing Mai's uncle again was a pleasure. He was her mother's brother. Mai was very close to him because she had lived with him as a child when her mother was not well enough to care for her. Mai's father had gone north seeking work.

After a short visit, we continued on to Mai's mother's grave. They had been working on it last year when we visited. The picture of her mother and some family names had been added. Mai was pleased. We all gathered around and paid our respects. I placed the flowers in the center of the monument. I could see the pain on Mai's face. She had not seen her mother again after she left in 1972. After the war it was impossible to communicate with anyone in Vietnam for many years. When Mai finally heard

Linda and Mai in the kitchen at Mai's cousin's house
(July 1997)

Ron, Nick, and Linda at dinner with Mai's cousin
(July 1997)

from a family member, her mother was dead. Much to her husband's dismay, she made her first trip back to Vietnam alone. She was devastated over losing her mother.

Another long and emotional day came to an end. It was time to say our good-byes. I felt sorry for Mai and her family because the visit was so brief. We had a slight problem with some intoxicated neighbors making themselves unwelcome in Mai's father's house. If Mai asked them to leave, they would come back after we had gone to retaliate! Her family would suffer, and we did not want that. We had to keep reminding ourselves that we were in Vietnam, not the United States.

Mai's sisters looked so sad as we drove away from the house. We hoped that everything would settle down and there would be no more problems for them. Mai left them clothes, household items, medicine, and money as usual.

We had to get going because it was getting late and we wanted to cross Hai Van Pass before dark.

Once back in Da Nang, we had an early dinner and went to bed. Mai went to see her father and uncle again.

Ron had been filming our stories the entire trip. It was time for him to return to Nha Trang. We wanted to go with him, but we still had work to do in Da Nang. We would catch up with him in Saigon on Wednesday. Ron had kept in touch with a Vietnamese woman he had met during the war. She lived in Switzerland now and came back to Nha Trang every summer to help with the family resort during the tourist season. What a special reunion for both of them.

Bright and early Monday morning, Nick and I were at the TV station. After some editing, the authorities approved my story for the air. The cost was forty dollars per night. They would show the pictures of Mary and her Vietnamese son and ask that viewers contact our hotel if they knew anything about them. The staff at the hotel had become very interested and involved in my plight.

I asked that my TV advertising run for two nights, Monday and Tuesday. They agreed. I paid them eighty dollars, and then

Mai, Linda, Ron, and Mai's family at the crash site in Quang Tri
(July 1997)

Mai, Linda, and Ron at Mai's mother's grave in Quang Tri
(July 1997)

we left the station to do some shopping and sightseeing. We were to go to Tam's house for dinner that night. I had to find her and tell her that we would be late because I wanted to stay at the hotel until after my story aired. The newspaper advertising was causing quite a stir, but we had not had any responses yet.

We sat on the edge of our beds in our hotel room anxiously waiting for Mary's picture to appear. When it appeared, my heart skipped a beat. I knew that everyone with a television would be seeing my story. The word would get back to someone that could help. I could only hope that it would happen in the next two days! We would be leaving Wednesday at 1:00 P.M. I had been faxing to the hotel for the past few months and they promised to get in touch with me in the United States if any information came in after our departure. Everyone has been so kind and helpful, but they do not understand why I was trying so hard to find this Vietnamese woman. It was very simple: Mickey loved her, and he wanted us to know her and love her. She was my family. If the situation were reversed and I had died, I know that my brothers and sister would do the same for me. We have a very special bond.

When we arrived at Tam's house, she was so excited. She had seen the advertising on her neighbor's television. Tam was genuinely happy for me.

We stayed close by the hotel on Tuesday but nothing happened. I was not discouraged. These things take time. Mai kept reminding me that things were different in Vietnam. She was sure that someone would come forward with some information. We had our final dinner in Da Nang before packing and getting ready to head back to Saigon. We would spend one night in Saigon before leaving for home.

Wednesday morning was hectic. Mai was up early to go visit her father one last time. I was getting ready to take a shower when the phone rang. The girl in the hotel lobby said that an old woman would be here in twenty minutes to tell me something about my brother. I almost fell over. Nick told me to calm down, to be realistic, and wait to hear what the woman had to say before I jumped to conclusions. I hated it when he got so logical!

It was the longest twenty minutes of my life, but finally the old woman arrived. The desk clerk translated for me in Mai's absence. This woman said that her neighbor was married to an Amerasian. He was in prison for no apparent reason. His mother's name was Hong Thi Chau. He was given up for adoption as an infant and raised by two Chinese women. His wife was on her way to the hotel with a picture of her husband's father. She was sure that his father was my brother.

We waited and waited, and then she appeared. She was a very pretty woman. She had one of her daughters with her. The little girl's hair was brown, her eyes were big, and she was very much the product of a mixed marriage. I wanted this young woman to be my brother's daughter-in-law. I wanted this little girl to come home with us and enjoy the life that was denied her father. I had to slow down and be rational. She did not have a picture of her husband's mother or father. She did have a picture of her husband. His hair was black, but his facial features resembled those of my family. It was amazing, but I was so confused. They had another daughter who was older and in school. I wanted to see both of the children. We gave her money for the cyclo ride to pick up her other daughter. These two little girls were adorable. I gave the young woman a self-addressed envelope and money for postage. She said she would get a picture from the Chinese women and send it to me. I told her that if the picture was a picture of my brother, I would come back to get them and see what I could do about her husband's prison term. We hugged and then cried as they left the hotel. I wondered if I would ever see them again. Meanwhile, Mai had returned from visiting her family. She could not believe the commotion in the lobby. An old woman had just come in claiming to be my sister-in-law. It was obvious that this woman was much too old to be Hong Thi Chau, but Mai talked to her and asked her a few questions anyway. She asked what her

American husband's name was. The woman said she did not know. She wanted Mai to tell her what his name was. Mai looked at Nick and I and said, "Fake." Comical as it was, I felt sorry for anyone who would go to such extremes to get out of his or her homeland.

Then the phone rang again, and the desk clerk said it was for "Miss Linda." The caller did not speak English, so the clerk took a message. The caller said that he had seen the TV advertisement and the pictures were of his sister and her son. He said they were living in Memphis and left the address. They hung up before I could ask for her phone number. I was in shock. Could this be my sister-in-law? Oh, how I hoped that it was true. I could not wait to get home.

A few minutes later, the man called again. Mai talked to him this time, but she said he was difficult to understand due to his accent. It seems that Vietnamese people have very different dialects.

He left a phone number this time. I guarded it with my life. I felt like a miracle was about to happen. I tried to imagine what I was going to say to this woman when I called her Friday morning. Could this really be Mary?

I had not given my brother's name to anyone. I had kept everything quiet. I just wanted to find Hong Thi Chau. She could then tell me all about my brother.

No one else came into the hotel Wednesday before we left. Nick and I went down the street for some lunch and privacy. We were so optimistic. We were also emotionally drained and could not wait to go home and follow up on the clues. I got what I came for, a clue, and maybe it would lead to Mary. If this clue wouldn't, then maybe the next would. I was positive that I would succeed. We had done things right this time.

On Wednesday evening, July 16th in Vietnam, Thursday, July 17th at home, Ron finally arrived via taxi at the hotel. We went to dinner and shared all the happenings of the day. Ron was elated for us. We asked him about his reunion. All went well, and he had filmed quite a bit in Nha Trang. We could not wait to see it when we got back home. We had a very enjoyable evening of dinner and conversation. Mai's father was doing much better, Nick and I were very pleased with the results of our labor, and Ron had a wonderful time in Nha Trang. We all had so much to be thankful for. I was thankful to have such good friends. There was a bond between us that was not present two weeks ago. We had experienced each other's lives.

On Thursday morning, July 17th in Saigon, we departed for home with emotions running wild. We arrived in Medford on Thursday, July 17th, at about midnight. We were exhausted. Our families were there to greet us. What a welcomed sight! I'm sure we were sorry sights after the long, long flight and the long, long layovers in Manila and San Francisco. But we were home, safe and sound.

It was well after 1:00 A.M. Friday morning before we arrived at the house. I was too wide-awake then so I listened to the thirteen messages on the answering machine. Nothing too important was there until I listened to the last message. It was from Hong Thi Chau! She said "Miss Linda, call me." I started to tremble. Nick told me to call right then, but I couldn't. It was 3:00 A.M. in Memphis.

We went to bed, but sleep would not come. Finally, at 4:00 a.m. I got up and made some coffee. Nick was soon to follow. He said, "Call her now." I told him that I had to get my thoughts together. I had to have all my questions planned out, and it was only 6:00 A.M. in Memphis.

Nick said that since it was Friday, she might be leaving for work soon so I had better call. So at 5:00 A.M. on Friday, July 18th, 1997, I picked up the phone and dialed the number that Mary had left on my answering machine. It was the same number I had been given in Vietnam. Nick was sitting beside me on the couch. My heart was pounding. The phone rang several times before a Vietnamese woman answered.

"Mary," I said. "This is Linda."

"Oh Linda," she said, and then there was silence.

I said, "Did you work in the officer's club in Da Nang?"

"No!" she said.

I thought I would die. Why did she say "No?" I thought she had worked in the officer's club in Da Nang. Then I remembered what Ross Perot had told me about facts. We must have assumed it was the officer's club in Da Nang because Mickey was an officer stationed there.

All of a sudden, she began to talk. She said "Linda, my husband, my Mickey, he die in Quang Tri, he helicopter pilot. He talk about Linda, Sandy, and his mama and daddy and brother. He tell me about Grandma in California. He love you very much."

The tears streamed down my face. Nick sat there with his arms around me. I listened as she went on and on about my brother, his family, and his dreams. I had found Mary! There was no doubt in my mind.

After I calmed down, I asked her about Mickey's child. She said the child was with her. I started to ask a lot of questions. She told me the child's name was Son. I was getting confused. Was it a boy or a girl? Mary started to back off. She told me that it had been a girl but someone had stolen her baby shortly after birth. She said that Mickey was very unhappy when he died because he had lost his baby.

Part of me just died. Then I composed myself and asked Mary if she would like me to help her find her baby girl. She said she would like that very much. We talked for a while longer, and I told her that I would be in Memphis soon to see her. I hung up the phone and cried my heart out! "Bittersweet" comes to mind again.

I had to call Sandy and tell her. She was ecstatic and devastated at the same time as were Nick and I. I spent the rest of the day in a dazed state.

About 5:00 P.M. Mary called me back. She was crying and apologizing. I asked her what was wrong. She said she had lied to me and was very sorry.

Mickey's baby was not stolen, and it was not a girl. Mary said that Mickey's son was with her in Memphis and his name was Son. She and Son were afraid that I was going to take him away from her so she had changed her story. I was a bit aggressive as I apologized. I told her that I would never try to tear her family apart. I just wanted them to know that they were not alone, that they were part of my family. I just wanted to love them. We cried and laughed. Son worked nights, so he was not at home, but she told me when to call to talk with him. They were not afraid of me anymore. I told her that I would be in Memphis on August 8. She insisted that I stay with her. I told her that my sister Sandy, my daughter Laurie, and her son Travis might come too. She said, "That's OK, you stay with me. We no sleep, we just sit up and talk."

I called Sandy again and shared yet another emotional conversation. We had to stop talking like that.

I found Mary, and I had found Son. I believe in miracles! My body and my mind were depleted of all energy. I had to get some sleep.

Nick was sound asleep, but my eyes were wide open. I could not rest. My body felt tired, but my mind wouldn't shut down.

I saw something in the hall, but I couldn't quite identify it. It was moving towards the bedroom. I wasn't afraid, I was relaxed. It moved through the bedroom and out the window, then appeared in the hall again only to retrace its steps. It was trying to get my attention so I could get a better look.

I stared right at it. Inside a black circle was a white figure. It kept circling through my bedroom. I got a good look as it passed by for the last time.

It was Mickey! He was smiling. He was so happy and proud of me for finding his family. I wanted to touch him but he was gone. I cried myself to sleep.

I believe in God.

On Saturday morning, I told Nick what had happened the night before. He seemed a little startled to hear me talking like that, but he was delighted that I had the experience.

On Sunday our friends Chuck and Joann came to visit. I shared my experience with them. Joann told me that I had seen an apparition. She told me that I would never see it again. Mickey came to let me know that he was all right now, that he could go and rest in peace.

Mickey, I'm sorry for making you wait twenty-four years.

Chapter Eight

Hong and Sons

During the next few conversations with Mary, she told me about her four sons. Her eldest son, Lam, had to remain in Vietnam.

Mary left Vietnam in 1991 through the Orderly Departure Program because she had an Amerasian son. She said the interview took only a couple of minutes in the early 1980s, but it had taken all those years to process their departure! By the time they were allowed to leave, Lam was over twenty one and had to be left behind. The child that had a ticket to leave the country in 1973 was now the only child left behind. Mickey had wanted to bring him home to be raised as one of his own.

After Mickey was shot down, Mary went home to Chu Lai to live with her parents. A couple of years later, she met a Vietnamese man who fathered her third son, Khanh. She found out that the father of her third son was already married and sent him on his way. She said she was not a home wrecker and told him to go back to his wife. Then she was a very young mother of three sons.

Mary had three brothers and three sisters. After her parents' death (they were both dead by 1975), it was her siblings who cared for her and her three sons. They worked hard in the rice fields and looked out for one another.

I could not wait to meet them. August 7th wasn't coming fast enough. I thought she might change her mind and not want us to come to Memphis. I tried very hard not to intimidate them or sound too aggressive.

Mary, Son, and Khanh had spent six months in the Philippines studying English before they were sponsored and flown to Memphis.

They must have been terrified when they arrived all alone in the United States. It would have been so different for all of us in 1973.

Mary went to work immediately upon her arrival in Memphis. She said she had a good boss. Mary remained employed by her sponsor until she became pregnant again. It was August of 1995 when Mary had her fourth son, Tommy. He was fathered by a neighborhood Vietnamese man. Son and Khanh supported their mother both emotionally and financially. Mary waited until Tommy was 2 years old to return to work. Her sponsor had to replace her, so she was now employed part-time in a market. They were a very close knit family.

On Thursday, August 7th, 1997, Laurie, her son Travis, and I left for Memphis. Sandy was having gallbladder problems and could not make the trip. We would fly all night, and arrive in Memphis at approximately 10:00 A.M. on Friday, August 8th.

Ron from Channel 12 TV in Medford had arranged for a TV station in Memphis to cover the reunion.

Finally, we landed in Memphis. We three fatigued travelers walked off the plane, but were not greeted by anyone. I saw a cameraman and a woman standing nearby. They were looking for someone but they seemed bewildered. I walked up and asked them if they were looking for Linda. They looked at me and said, "Yes."

"I'm Linda. Where is my Vietnamese family?" I was devastated. They were not there.

Laurie and I discussed the possibilities, and then I went to call their home. There was no answer. They were probably on their way, so we waited, but no one showed up.

Plan "B" went into action: I would page them. Maybe they went to the wrong gate.

Shortly after the page, we saw two Asians walking towards. At first I did not think it was them (I was not wearing my glasses), but Laurie assured me it was. She was right!

I ran up to Mary and hugged her, and cried and hugged her again. She was so tiny. Then she introduced me to Son. He was so bashful and looked scared. The poor young man had these big American women hanging all over him, hugging him and kissing him. He was the perfect gentleman. He just stood there and took it with a smile.

After things calmed down and the TV crew wiped their eyes, we agreed to a short interview. Mary and Son were so accommodating. They spoke English fairly well. Oh, I wish Mickey was there to see us.

We walked together, hand in hand, to the baggage claim. There were no bags to be found. Everyone was gone. We had been at the gate so long that our luggage had been taken upstairs. After retrieving our belongings, Son escorted us to the van that would take us home.

We talked and talked on the short drive home. We had a lot to catch up on. As I looked at Son, I could see the family resemblance. I wondered if I was just imagining a resemblance, or if he really did remind me of Mickey. His hair and eyes were dark, but he still looked like Mickey. Something about the shape of his eyes and forehead reminded me of my brother. His hands were long and bony, just like my son Brian's. He walked like my uncle. His kindness and soft voice were Mickey's.

Mary told me many times that all her boys were good like Mickey. "He was a good man," she said. We knew that.

When we arrived at their small apartment in Memphis, Son and Mary carried our things inside. They treated us like royalty. I think they were as happy to meet us as we were to meet them.

The apartment complex was in a run-down neighborhood inhabited mainly by Vietnamese and Negroes. The hallway leading to their apartment was dark and in need of repairs. I got nervous when thinking about the catastrophes that could take place in this building. I worried about my family and others in the building. The occupants of the building all seemed nice and friendly. They were close and helped one another out by baby-sitting, lending their cars to whomever needed one, exchanging food items, and basically caring about one another. It was a community within a community! I was relieved to know that

Mary and Travis

Linda and Son

Linda and Mary

Tommy

Son and Travis

Khanh and Son

"Mary" Hong Thi Chau in Memphis
(1997)

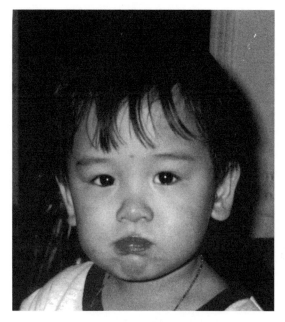

Tommy, Mary's youngest son
(2 years old, 1997)

Khanh, Mary's third son
(21 years old, 1997)

they had such good friends. It was obvious that they protected one another.

Mary was in the middle of preparing for Tommy's second birthday party. It was going to be a large get together.

It didn't take long before the neighbors started to show up to see us. We were exhausted from the flight, but did manage to stay awake most of the day. Son had to go to work at 4 P.M. People were in and out all day. As usual, we were greeted warmly by everyone. No one could believe that I had searched for so long to find Mary. I was so glad that I had not given up. I sat and watched them scurry about, waiting on us, smiling at us, but I wanted them to sit down and talk! They were the busiest people I had ever seen. I felt like I was back in Da Nang, but I was in Memphis.

Our stay was going to be short. It was already Friday afternoon, and we had to be at the airport by 1:00 p.m. Sunday. I was already dreading good-byes. Every time I looked into their eyes, I wanted to cry. Their life was supposed to be so different. I apologized to Son for not finding them many years earlier. He took my hand and said, "That's OK, Linda, we have you now." When he touched my hand, I knew it was the hand of Mickey.

Tommy was asleep at the neighbors when we arrived at the apartment, and Khanh was working until 8:00 P.M. Mary was squatting on the kitchen floor preparing Vietnamese specialties for Tommy's birthday. Son left for work, and Laurie, Travis, and I took a nap.

We woke refreshed, but Mary looked exhausted! She was still squatting and cooking. Laurie helped out with wrapping and tying the banana leaves around the sticky rice and meat mixture. I was proud of Laurie. It was a real culture shock for her, but she never complained.

Tommy finally woke up and came home. He is such a cute, little guy a few months older than Travis. They got along fairly well and spent quite a lot of time in the hallway riding toddler toys and racing. We were always close by.

Khanh arrived home shortly after eight. He is much more outgoing than Son. He wanted us to sing Karaoke! We declined but he sang a few songs for us. He has a beautiful soft voice. He said that Son sang also. Khanh is a nail technician in a salon, so he talks to women all day long. Son is an attendant in a parking facility across the street from Elvis Presley's Memphis Restaurant, so he sits in solitude the majority of the time. They both work six days a week, taking off only on Sundays.

Son called me from work and we talked for nearly an hour, stopping briefly when a customer pulled up to the booth. It was a special time for us both. I had a difficult time believing that I was talking to Mickey's son.

Before I left Medford, I wrote Mary's name, address, and phone number in my Rolodex. It sounds silly, but it was so emotional. It was just as emotional as it was twenty-four years ago when I took my brother's name out of my Rolodex! I could now call them, write to them, send them a card or package, or visit them whenever I wanted. I felt Mickey's presence once again.

Mary places food on the table for Mickey every time they eat. She has been doing it for twenty-four years. She laughs and talks about Mickey as if he were standing next to us. She said that Mickey talks to her every day, and that he looks out for her and the boys. Mary always refers to Mickey as her husband.

Our airport reunion aired Friday evening, but we missed it. Saturday, a woman who had worked with Mary when she first arrived in Memphis, called to tell her how happy she was that I had found her. Mary handed the phone to me. This woman said that Mary had talked about Mickey all the time. Some of her friends tried to encourage her to look for us, but no one knew how to go about performing the task. This woman said that if ever there was a human being that deserved a break, it was Hong. (We are the only ones that call her Mary.) She said that Hong and her boys are good people. It was easy to see why Mickey loved Mary.

Before Son went to work on Saturday, he took Laurie, Travis

and me on a tour of Memphis. We wanted to go see the newly opened Elvis Presley's Memphis Restaurant, but we had to wait for an hour or so before they let anyone else in. It was raining, so we opted to find a café and have some coffee.

I was sitting directly across from Son when I took his hand and asked him if he knew what a MIA/POW bracelet was. He did not know. I showed him the bracelet on my wrist bearing Mickey's name. He gently touched it and smiled. I took it off my wrist and placed it on his. Son read the inscription, rubbed the bracelet and covered it with his sleeve as to protect it. I had been wearing that bracelet since it was given to me on July 4th, 1996. Now it was home where it belonged. Laurie, Son, and I looked at each other and smiled.

We left the café to take our places in line. While we were waiting to enter Elvis Presley's Restaurant, a woman pointed to us and said, "I saw y'all on TV last night."

Son left for work about 3:30 P.M. on Saturday. Khanh would be home from work at 8:00 P.M. The guests for Tommy's party started to arrive about 6:00 P.M.

Mary had prepared a feast! There were numerous traditional Vietnamese dishes, French bread, barbecued ribs, rice, of course, and the all-American birthday cake.

The guests were all Vietnamese, some English speaking and some not. Most of the guests brought envelopes with money inside as Tommy's gift. He received only one present that was not money, and only one other child attended the party besides Tommy and Travis.

We all gathered around the table chatting. Mary would translate for the non-English speaking guests. Everyone was so happy to meet us, and the feeling was mutual. That tiny apartment was filled with so much love. The party went on for a few hours. It looked like Mary had enough food left for two more gatherings. Many of the guests left with food, as was their custom.

Our visit was almost over. We would be on our way home by midday tomorrow.

After everyone left and the table was cleared, we sat for awhile and talked. Mary told me that Mickey bought her Salem cigarettes and yellow gum (Juicy Fruit) and she would cook for him. She said that he loved her cooking. Mickey told her that when they arrived in the United States she would never have to work again. He wanted her to stay home and take care of the babies and cook. She laughed when she told me because she did not understand how it would be possible for a wife to stay home. She said she told Mickey she would take care of him. I knew she meant every word.

Mary also told me that my grandmother in California had written to her and Mickey and had sent a picture of her house and told them that it would be theirs when they came home. She asked about the rest of the family and wished that they were all there to meet her.

Mary said she was in Saigon getting her physical and papers to leave the country when Mickey was shot down. She told me that they had gotten married at a hotel in Da Nang with a few friends present. They lived in a small apartment. Mickey would come to see her every night when he was off duty. When she returned from Saigon, she waited for Mickey, but he did not come. She said she heard his footsteps in the hall, but when she opened the door no one was there. She cried and did not know what to do. After two or three nights, she could not stand it anymore. Mary went to the Main Gate and asked for Mickey. A colonel and another officer came to the gate and told Mary that her husband had been killed in Quang Tri. She accused them of killing Mickey. She said that Mickey was not supposed to fly anymore but one of the pilots had not felt well so the colonel asked Mickey to fly. Of course Mickey said yes.

Mary said she had collapsed while screaming and crying. She and her two boys had tickets for the United States. She did not know what to do, so she ran home to her parents. She was not going to go to the United States without her husband.

Mickey had told her that he would leave a couple of days before her and the children. In the last letter Mickey wrote to

Sandy, he had said that very same thing. He also said that he was taking them to Disneyland. Mickey was a big kid at heart. I think that's why kids loved him so much.

Even though twenty-four years have passed, I still find it difficult to believe that Mickey is gone.

Sunday morning arrived too quickly. Everyone had the day off so we did get to spend some time together. Son and I went for a ride. I wanted to buy them an answering machine because they were never home and I had such a difficult time reaching them. Before we got to the store, Son took me to his cousin's house. I was excited to know that they had other relatives in the area, but they were not really cousins. They just referred to one another as such! I had met his cousin last night at the party. We sat in the living room and visited for a while before continuing on to the store.

While Son was driving, I looked over at him and smiled. I knew Mickey was watching us. Who would have ever believed this would be happening? Tears started to form in my eyes, but I managed to blink them away. I would save my tears for the airport. I did not want to cry then because I was too happy.

I tried to explain DNA testing to Son. I think he understood. I told him as far as I was concerned, he was my nephew, but that I would like to get the DNA testing done so that I could prove it to others. If he was indeed my nephew, he should be entitled to some benefits.

It is quite obvious that he is an Amerasian. If he was not my nephew, then he is someone else's nephew, and I would help him find the truth. He is Mary's son, as are Lam, Khanh, and Tommy. Any son of my sister-in-law is a nephew of mine. I love them all. They are an extraordinary family.

I assured Son that I would never do anything he did not want me to do. I was not here to disrupt their lives, I just wanted to enhance it if they would allow me the privilege. Son said he would do whatever I wanted him to do.

As soon as we arrived in the apartment, Son disappeared. We had to leave for the airport soon, so I hoped he would not be gone long. While we were gone, Khanh had taken Laurie and Travis to the Vietnamese market.

We told Mary that we had better go to the airport. She sent Khanh to find Son. It wasn't long before they both returned. Son had a flower pinned to his collar – he had been at the temple. He was such a wonderful, spiritual young man. I wondered what was going through his mind. I had been searching for them for two years, and then I just popped into their lives one day.

We all piled into the van and headed for the airport. We were all fairly quiet. I had a knot in my stomach.

The boys carried our luggage, while I checked in at the counter. They took Laurie and Travis to the Cinnamon Bun Shop and told me to join them there when I was finished. We all had coffee and a cinnamon bun while we chatted.

I heard them announce our flight. It was time to go. We all stood up, cleared our table, and headed for the gate.

I took one last look at my family and burst into tears. I hugged each one and told them that I loved them. They said they loved me too. They promised to come and visit. I just could not let go of them. When Son hugged Laurie, I could see his face, and he looked like he had just lost his best friend. Laurie told me that he did not want to let go of her either. I went around one more time with hugs and good-byes before Laurie pulled me away. "It's time to go, Mom," she said as she took my hand and guided me to the jetway.

I did not understand how it was possible to be so happy and so sad at the same time. The word "bittersweet" came to mind once again.

Chapter Nine

The Beginning

The search is over but it is the beginning of a new odyssey.

When I stop and realize exactly what has happened these past two years, I know that it was nothing short of a miracle! I was guided down the path to success by Mickey and encouraged by those who Mickey chose to support me. He knows who I respect and listen to. He knew exactly what he was doing.

I did what any loving sister would do if she were in my shoes. We are all put on this earth for a purpose. I must go on from here, because my job is not complete.

I had been reading, asking questions, and studying about DNA testing ever since I found out about Mickey's child. I knew the day would come when I would need the help of a DNA laboratory.

I went first to the U.S. Army for assistance. They referred me to some private laboratories around the country. I had read a book by Dr. Maples and had also heard quite a bit about him. I called the laboratory in Florida only to find out that he had passed away in February 1997. I really thought that he could help me, but now I had to turn elsewhere. But where?

I really needed some guidance. I had no remains of my brother, nothing from which to pull any DNA from except an envelope! Can anyone, or should I say, will anyone try to help? I know the envelope is old, twenty-five years old, but it's all we have right now. I called a couple of labs and really did not have much luck. One day I called LabCorp in Burlington, North Carolina, and talked to some "real people."

The woman who answered the phone listened to my story.

She was so kind and caring. She said, "This is the sort of thing that people do for one another." She told me to call back on Monday and talk to the manager, who was not in that day.

I did call back and left a message. It took a couple of phone calls, but finally I was put in touch with Jessica. She talked to the manager, and they decided to help me with my plight. I started to cry. These truly were "real people."

Since we had no remains of my brother from which to draw DNA, we had a problem. Sandy had an envelope that had come from Mickey just before we lost him in 1973. I had read that DNA could be extracted from saliva off the back of a postage stamp in some cases. I was hoping for another miracle. Could they get my brother's DNA from the envelope?

Jessica said that they would try. She mailed all the appropriate paperwork, return envelopes, and documentation to collect the specimen from me. I only sent part of the envelope because I wanted to keep some for identification purposes. I mailed everything back as soon as was humanly possible.

Several weeks went by, and Jessica called periodically to keep me posted on their progress. They were not successful in pulling any DNA out of the envelope at their lab so they sent it to another branch of LabCorp. Jessica said that if anyone could get something out of that envelope, they could. I waited, but not patiently.

Finally, Jessica called. The news was not good. They could not pull anything from the envelope. There was nothing there. We were so disappointed.

I guess I am only allowed one miracle per year. I will have to wait a little longer. Maybe Mickey's remains will come home someday, or maybe technology will improve and I can try again. I have waited twenty-five years to find these people, so I can wait for another miracle to come my way.

In the meantime, I will bask in the glory and enjoy my new-found family. Mickey knows the truth and the answers to my questions. He will let me know what to do next. I really need a rest right now.

When I look back at the last two years, I see nothing but happiness.

The Vietnam War was so tragic and ugly, but underneath the ugliness and sorrow, there is beauty, love, forgiveness, and hope.

I went to visit the Vietnam Memorial in 1988. As Nick and I approached the wall hand-in-hand, he said that I pulled back as though I did not want to see it. When we finally reached the wall, I was surprised by what I felt. I was overwhelmed with grief only for a moment. I realized that Mickey was in a special, peaceful, beautiful place with all his comrades and former enemies. They had forgiven and so must we so we can join them some day.